Slaves of Rapparee

(The Wreck of *The London*)

Pat Barrow

Edward Gaskell *publishers*
DEVON

First published 1998 by
EDWARD GASKELL Publishers
6 Grenville Street
Bideford • Devon
EX39 2EA

ISBN 1 -898546 - 25 - 8

Slaves of Rapparee
(The Wreck of *The London*)

by

Pat Barrow

Typeset, printed & bound by
The Lazarus Press
Unit 7 Caddsdown Business Park
Bideford
Devon EX39 3DX

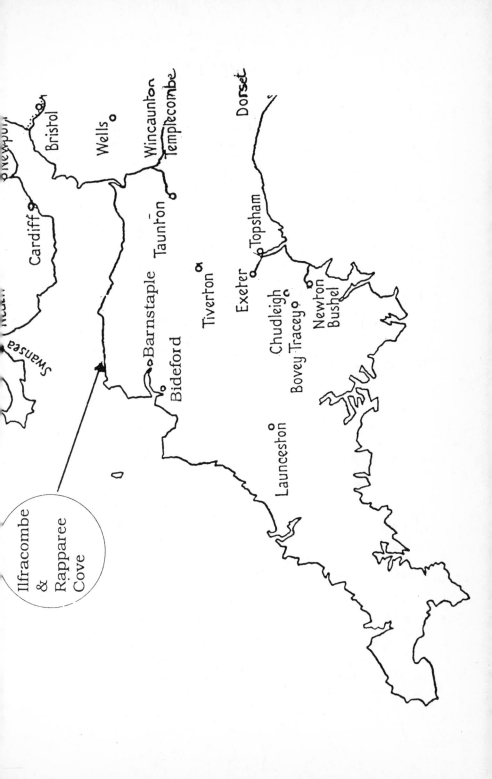

Acknowledgements

I must first thank my wife Rosamund for sticking by me – and helping me in and during the digging, and the traumatic times that followed. Her help in every way was invaluable especially in dealing with the mountain of correspondence which arrived daily when the media interest was at its zenith. Many thanks to my step daughter Christine for her help with video footage – and for making endless cups of tea.

My thanks must go to Diane Upton for her support and her belief that the book would be published. Also Joy Slocombe, whose warm welcome and guidance I certainly needed at various times throughout the controversy. Her unwavering loyalty will always be remembered by me; as will that of Jeanne Hardwick whose loyalty was also unquestionable throughout the whole controversy – the much needed new evidence came from her friends in London, and in this respect I would like to express my gratitude to Eileen Weston and her associates, for their tireless enthusiasm.

The help of Jeanne's husband, George, was greatly appreciated on the first excavation – his willingness to help was second to none. I would also like to thank all other members of Ilfracombe Museum, past and present, for helping me with my enquiries. Also the staff of the North Devon Athenaeum, and the National Maritime Museum for their patient help. Also I must thank my 'number one digging buddy' from years ago, Ron Jewell. I would also like to thank all those people who found coins in the cove and gave me the details for the story, and in particular Keith Harker, Brian Bradshaw, Brian Forrest, and Nick Pugsley. I would also like to thank Margaret Reed, and Richard Ashford, for their help and for the advice I had to seek at the height of the controversy. Also all those people who helped with the first excavation.

I would also like to thank Bernie Grant MP, whose help and interest in the site gave me renewed inspiration – a special thanks to his staff and friends. Also I would like to thank those members of various councils who helped to bring together meetings on the issues of the cove. I would particularly like to thank Joy Slocombe and the trustees at Ilfracombe Museum for letting me use the picture of *The London*, featured on the front cover.

Contents

This book is dedicated to
Rosamund

*The condition upon which God hath given liberty to man
is eternal vigilance.*

Introduction

On a Sunday evening in October 1796 a British transport *The London* foundered in a violent storm as it approached the harbour of Ilfracombe on the North Devon coast. It went to the bottom of the sea just outside Rapparee Cove and on board were more than 100 black prisoners from the West Indies. Also on board was a vast amount of gold coins and jewellery, the fate of which has always been unclear.

Fifty years after the wreck, one of the great scientists of the 19th century, Phillip Gosse FRS, friend of Darwin and Kingsley, attested to the presence of the bones still visible where they had been hastily buried in the cove close to the rocks. Gosse also revealed that not all of those on board had perished. In 1856 fitful articles and letters to the press, particularly the *Illustrated London News* continued to remind an indifferent world of the terrible incident.

I became aware of an increasing hostility as my research began to uncover details which it was obvious some people would rather I had left alone. While the motive for transporting black prisoners *from* the Caribbean islands to a Bristol prison intrigued me, it appeared to infuriate the powers-that-be. The media seized upon the idea that this was a slave ship, yet it was never that simple. I was encouraged to describe the victims as *prisoners-of-war* as they were clearly freedom fighters embroiled in the Napoleonic & French Revolutionary wars which at the time were raging in the West Indies.

Yet these people had fought heroically to *avoid* slavery, and had been captured by the British. So what of the survivors; what became of the people who did not perish in the wreck of *The London*? Were they ultimately treated honourably, as prisoners-of-war – or as *slaves*?

Pat Barrow

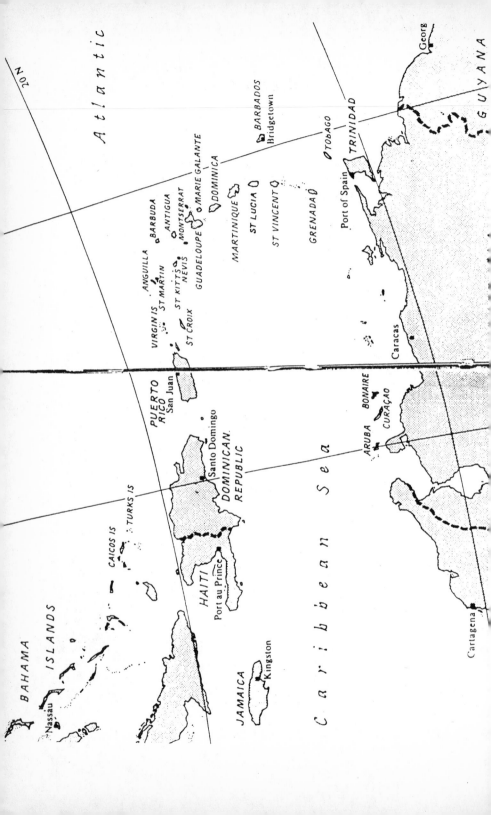

1

A Personal Story

I became interested in ship wrecks in about 1970, and thought about taking up sub-aqua diving, in order to find them. I had aspirations of finding a wreck, which I hoped would have all its contents undisturbed and complete. A veritable time capsule, like an undiscovered room lain frozen in time and waiting to be unlocked. But what I dreamt most of all was to find such a shipwreck and uncover the *story* behind it, leading me further back in time as I devoured book after book on the history and natural history of the coasts of Devon.

My quest eventually led me to a book written by Phillip Henry Gosse entitled *A Naturalist's Rambles on the Devonshire Coast* which was dated 1853. The heading that aroused my curiosity was "Treasure Ship Wreck At Ilfracombe" and Gosse wrote:

> '...two transports returning from the West Indies.... for years after the sad event, the people of the town used to find gold coins, and jewels among the shingle at low tide.'

PH Gosse, I later discovered, was a distinguished Naturalist (see page 119) and his credentials are beyond question – there could be no doubt that there *was* a shipwreck at Ilfracombe in the 1790s.

I found myself faced with a number of puzzles: If, as Gosse states, 'most of the people on board were saved...' *how many* perished, and where are they buried? What were the names of the 'two transports' and where bound? Were both ships wrecked; or only one? Who found the gold coins and jewels? What type of gold coins were they? Incredibly, as it turned out, people were *still find-ing* them.

Discussing the floor of the cove and its composition Gosse commented:

> ....the observant stranger notices a quantity of yellow gravel, scattered all along the water-line between tide marks. This at once strikes him as a remarkable feature, seeing that nothing of the kind is found on other parts of this coast, nor does any analogous formation exist in the vicinity.
>
> On enquiry he learns that these yellow pebbles are strangers, and not native of the place; that they are, in fact, the enduring records of a tragical event that occurred some fifty years ago......
>
> .....The vessels were ballasted with this yellow gravel, which though washed to and fro by the rolling surf, remains to bear witness of this shipwreck, and to identify the spot where it took place; a curious testimo-ny, which probably will endure long after the event itself is lost in oblivion....

I have since seen this yellow gravel or ballast for myself, but at the time of reading my thoughts were that here was the very story I could rescue from oblivion — and I set out to do so.

§

After much research, my questions began to appear impossible to answer. The details I sought were not recorded; the very things I wanted to know were not there to be found. I felt a strange sense of remorse — the knowledge I sought was lost to posterity. It *should* have have been recorded. It was unbelievably frustrating.

I subsequently guessed that the finders of the gold coins and jewels were not inclined to tell — or record such details — for more reasons than one. The prudent population of North Devon have never been accused of a lack of providence and the fishing and beachcombing communities are positively acute. They were inclined to keep such things secret – locations which had passed from generation to generation for over 200 years were not to be revealed lightly. I was once asked, 'Would *you* disclose a free source of wealth?'

Thus I persevered with my solitary search through what records there were. Details of the various wrecks mentioned became ever more confusing and yet had the curious effect of motivating me; my adrenaline flowed with an almost desperate desire to solve this problem – a desire which sometimes worried me in its intensity. I was fuelled by an immense determination.

In 1971 I was living in Barnstaple, my native town, which is about eleven miles from the resort of Ilfracombe on the North Devon Coast. I decided I would visit Rapparee Cove and inspect the area of the shipwreck. The sea was as clear as gin, and the whole setting a picture on that sunny June morning as I walked amongst the shingle finding nothing but seaweed and stones. I had often pondered as to the speed with which the wreck must have broken up, imagining this huge ship being mercilessly dashed against the rocks. The violence of the storms which often visit themselves upon Ilfracombe are an exhilarating and awe-inspiring sight. Still, I wondered that there was no physical structural evidence of the ship left, even in Gosse's day. At the time I can remember imagining just how many other people over the years had come to this particular location, perhaps in search of treasure, only to find the same as I had found – nothing but seaweed and stones.

However, this was what I had expected . Many people, of course, have explored the cove since the wreck took place, especially in the past when the rumours of the gold coins and jewels were more widely known. The cove is a regular digging place for beachcombers, and I conceded it likely that anything worth finding had been found long ago. So back to the conflicting and confusing records I went, hoping that somehow I might be able to establish the name of the ship or ships if both mentioned by Gosse had wrecked. The idea that this mystery must be solved was intensifying. I had to admit it was fast becoming an obsession.

§

In the *Transactions of the Devonshire Association*, vol.
XI, 1879, P.167. Mrs Slade-King writes:
> '...a Bristol ship with slaves on board. Their corpses
> were denied Christian burial, and their skulls are even
> now at times turned up in the neighbouring fields.
> Tradition says that many of them were drowned with
> iron fetters on their legs.'

This was an interesting piece of information.
Unfortunately Mrs Slade-King did not name the wreck
concerned, yet added the intriguing detail about actual
people who died on the wreck. At the time, my research
skills had not advanced far enough to enable me to link
the bodies talked of by Mrs Slade-King with any wreck in
particular. I was further confused when I found mention
of another possibility in *The Coasts of Devon and Lundy
Island, 1895* by J L W Page. He wrote:
> 'In Rapparee Cove drove ashore one of the prizes
> taken by Lord Rodney in an engagement with the
> French and Spanish. She became a total wreck , and
> for years the skulls of the prisoners and some of the
> treasure in the shape of coins were picked up on the
> beach. It is said that many of these skulls were of
> Negroes, so the engagement must have been that of
> 1782, when Rodney defeated the Compte de Grasse.'

By this time I was convinced that of the 'two transports'
mentioned by Gosse only one had been wrecked.
Fortunately I was able to find the names of the prizes
taken by Lord Rodney at the Battle of 'Les Saintes' on
12th April in 1782. These details are recorded in *The
History of the British Navy*, on page 338. The book states
that there were six prizes taken:
> 'The Ville de Paris', 'The Hector', and 'The Glorious'
> went down with the whole of their crews on the way
> back to England, but 'The Caton' was driven back in a
> hopeless state to the American coast, and of the glori-
> ous 12th April, 'The Jason' and 'The Ardent' were the
> only trophies which reached England, accompanied by
> three of Rodney's ships.'

Thus *The Jason* and *The Ardent* became two possible
names for the wreck concerned.

Sketches at Ilfracombe from the *Illustrated London News*

13

This led me to Richard Larn's book, *Devon Shipwrecks* where he writes:

'....a large ship was ashore in 1782, said to have been one of the prizes of Lord Rodney. A vessel returning from the West Indies with black prisoners was driven ashore at Ilfracombe early in the 19th century with gold and silver coins in connection with the wreck.'

He also mentions the 'yellow gravel ballast', referred to by Gosse. However Richard Larn goes on to suggest that the reports may have been referring to the transport *The London*, carrying British troops and French prisoners of war, 'lost in Rapparee Cove on 9th October 1796'. This account did at least agree with Gosse in parts, and also gives a name to the wreck. However, Larn also writes of three other possibilities, one of which was the *Arms of Bristol* which sank in 1676, which at a glance partly supports Mrs Slade-King who wrote that the wreck was a Bristol ship.

Larn also writes:

'a rich Spanish ship came ashore during a gale, in a cove once outside the harbour but now enclosed by the breakwater.'

This wreck confuses the issue further because rich Spanish ships and gold coins tend to be inseparable in peoples' minds. Still, this ship had to be considered as a contender. Richard Larn also suggests that the Spanish ship may have been one of the prizes of Lord Rodney. Finally he writes of

...'The Nostra Seignora de Bon Successo' of Lisbon, stranded at our harbour's mouth and went to pieces.'

This was on 2nd October 1780, a wreck that was finally ruled out by the dating evidence of a coin (1784) found by Brian Bradshaw at a later date.

These accounts indicate just how confusing the whole issue had become, with plenty of possible candidates, but no firm evidence of the name of the wreck. Thus the recorded evidence tended to leave me literally high and dry.

§

In January 1973 I had a chance to take a close look at the seabed, in forty feet of water, just off the mouth of Rapparee Cove. The visibility was a poor 2-4 feet and all I saw at the time was sand, rock, mud and shingle, in the freezing cold water of the harbour. This did nothing to quench my curiosity and I returned to the cove many times during the intervening years.

§

In 1978, my long standing friend Ron Jewell, and I visited Rapparee after violent storms had cast up the shingle against the wall at the back of the cove. The severity of these storms had uncovered the larger rocks buried below and left older, sunken objects much nearer the surface and thus much more likely to be discovered.

2

The Treasure in the Cove

On Saturday 14th January 1978, Ron Jewell rang me to tell me that he had just seen a *Westward Diary* news report on television about two schoolboys called Peter Richards and Andrew Douse who had found, among other items, a gold coin dated 1725 in Rapparee Cove. I was convinced this had to be one of the actual coins referred to in the various books and represented the breakthrough I had long sought.

With Ron, I set off from Barnstaple in my ex-army Land Rover to find out more and as we were driving down into Ilfracombe we encountered a fully saddled horse running loose toward us along the road. As this was an obvious danger I stopped the Land Rover to let the horse pass before driving on. We soon encountered the fully kitted and dejected rider of the horse walking along the road, and again stopped to see if we could help. It was decided to turn the Land Rover around in the road, and pursue the horse which we eventually – and very carefully – overtook. Stopping in front of it, the owner alighted from our vehicle and walked up to the horse very gingerly, and caught it. He then walked to his horse-box, which was parked nearby at Plaistow quarry.

After the rider had thanked us both we continued on and parked in the car-park near Larkstone cove, just along from Rapparee. We then unloaded our equipment and began to walk along the path. We were nearly in view of the steps at the top of the entrance to Rapparee, when we met a man who engaged us in conversation. He told us about the coin that had been found and expressed a doubt regarding the coin's value, which the

TV report had suggested could be one thousand pounds. The turn our conversation was taking began to annoy me because whenever coins are mentioned, value always comes top of the list of questions. To me the untold story which I knew lay behind the discovery of this coin – the shipwreck itself — was worth more than gold; I desired it more.

Ron and I continued along the winding path, and stopped in the seated area at the top of the steps which overlook the mouth of the cove. Several people were in the cove searching and generally milling around. The news of the gold coin find was spreading fast and the activities taking place below clearly indicated the level of interest which had now been aroused. So we continued, and started to search near the waterline, which was low and therefore near the mouth of the cove. This seemed a natural place to start assuming that any ship wrecked here would not get beyond this point – and the accounts given regarding coins found appeared to point to their location as low water. This gave the impression of being low down the cove, near the low tide mark. We searched on the left side, just above the low tide line, and found nothing.

We then decided to try the high tide mark area, and whilst we were there a young lad told us that he had seen Peter Richards find the coin and that he had made his find in the centre of the cove. First Peter had found an octagonal three pence or sixpence, and then got another signal from his detector in the same hole, which turned out to be the gold coin dated 1725 (When I had a chance to examine this coin, at a later date, I could see that it was a Portuguese Joanna piece, of John V (1706-50), with a very wide edge knock).

At 4pm Ron and I saw Keith Harker and his father Robin, find another gold Joanna coin dated 1723. The location this time was central – between a quarter and a third of the way down the cove from the cliff face. We were digging a hole about five metres from them, and had found some modern coins but the tide was now coming in fast, and the light was failing.

It was about 5pm when we left the cove to return home to Barnstaple. On the way home, I tried to persuade Ron to return to the cove with me that night, after the tide had receded, but his girlfriend was cooking supper for him so he declined. A strong feeling told me that more coins lay still buried in the cove and this, coupled with an overwhelming and burning desire to return to Rapparee that night was to prove a compulsion too powerful to resist.

That evening it was difficult to while away the time. I tried to watch a John Wayne cowboy film which was on TV but felt distracted. In my mind I was still in the cove and I waited anxiously picturing the tide as it came fully in. At 10pm I returned to Rapparee, quickly completing the twelve mile journey on the back road to Combe [a local name for Ilfracombe] encountering very little traffic on the way.

When I arrived in the cove car park, and turned off the Land Rover lights it immediately became apparent just how dark it really was. After negotiating the winding path to the cove, I carefully descended the steep cove steps laden with my gear – which included a Second World War trench shovel, and an oil lamp to light my way. The lamp had to be carefully lit, but there was no wind and the match burned easily.

Arriving at the bottom of the steps I was shocked to find that there was only just enough dry shingle at the high tide mark to stand on. This disappointed me considerably, but I hurried on down to the cove hoping that the tide would recede enough by the time I arrived – of course, it didn't. I was hoping to get far enough down the cove through the central region where a triangular rock stood on its edge, marking the spot where Keith Harker and his father had dug earlier. I could see the rock, it was just five metres in front of me. I was so close, and yet so far away, with the natural barrier of the sea between myself and the rock. Rather than wait for time to go by while the water receded, I started to dig a hole at the spot where I stood, with the waves just licking my boots, about two metres from the cliff face. The oil lamp fumes and the poor light strained my eyes, but I noticed that I could clearly see the triangular rock, due now to the low cloud reflecting the lights of Ilfracombe. I reasoned that if I could see the rock, then perhaps I did not need the light of the oil lamp, so I blew it out, and in less than a minute – to my relief – I could see quite well. Behind me I could see the fissure in the rocks at the cliff base, a location about six or eight metres from the

18

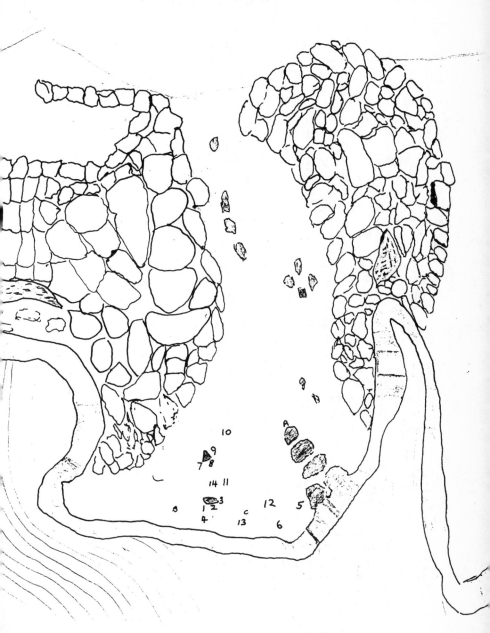

Map indicating location of various finds

natural, beach stone wall, which was on the far side of the cove. I dug the pit deeper, in 100mm layers, all the time stood in water, the waves crashing in around me.

Gradually the tide receded and the water in the hole became less of a problem, with only a small amount of fresh water present, which flows through the cove from the field above. In fact, the beach became almost dry as the tide receded and I could soon see all of the triangular rock where Keith had been digging. However, by this time I was more interested in my new location, which I was systematically digging. At first I found a few modern coins, until I reached a fine sandy layer that may have been composed of iron panning as it coloured the fine sand a gingery red.

It was in this layer that I found my first gold coin. I could see in the faint ambient light, cast from the low cloud, that the coin I held in my hand was a light colour. It was heavy for its size and thus I knew it was gold even before I had struck a match to see it clearly for the first time. I was astounded when I saw the date – 1720. I had sorted each handful of sand on top of a flat rock; the rock helped because it contrasted the colours in the poor light, against which my eyes were straining all the time. Still, it was better than breathing the nauseating oil lamp fumes. Ecstatic with excitement, and with the coin in my hand, I stopped and thought about who was the last person to have touched the coin. It may have been a captain, or a rich gentleman, who knows....

Taking the coin, I placed it on a low ledge in the rock crevice for safe keeping. It was a Portuguese 4000 reis, of John V, and I had found it shortly before midnight. By 12.30am I had found two more gold coins — a British James II guinea, dated 1686, — and another 4000 reis, dated 1689. The latter coin was in *extremely good* condition; the first two in *very good* condition and considering the rough seas that must have thundered over them for all those years this was remarkable. By the time I had examined the coins, the excitement of the evening and the strain on my eyes had left me very tired. However I felt a sense of achievement – fulfilled and ready to leave, I retrieved the coins from the rock crevice taking one more look over to the triangular rock. I thought in my contentment, 'I've had enough for tonight,' – the triumphant end to a long day.

With the coins carefully placed in my pocket, I made my way cautiously across the shingle and over the rugged rocks in that dark treacherous angle of the cove to the steps, which I struggled up with all my gear, suddenly feeling very weary. By the time I reached the top I could hardly keep my eyes open although the adrenaline in my thirty year old body was still flowing and I struggled on laden with all my gear. I became more alert as the Land Rover lights were switched on, and the engine roared into life and I drove home to Barnstaple feeling elated, arriving home at 2am to surprise my wife with the news of my find.

When I reached into my pocket to show her the coins, they jangled together and I was brought down to earth with the thought that, after all, they were really only money.

Ring of Bells, Ilfracombe. JC.

3

The Sunday Gold Rush
Rapparee Cove

The following day was Sunday, 15th January 1978, and I called around again to see my friend Ron, who thought he could tell by my expression that I had found some of the coins. Of course, being my usual self, I tantalised him for a while, keeping him guessing whether I had or not.

Ron had arranged for us to see another friend Derek Monk, who was very excited when we called around to meet him at his place. We travelled together back to Rapparee and arrived at the cove to find 22 people digging furiously for gold – the 1978 *Sunday Gold Rush* had begun. There was an interesting assortment of people of all ages scattered around; one elderly couple were using a garden sieve, an unlikely tool, because most of the shingle was too big to go through the holes. Another man called Michael Mackie paid a day worker, Kenny, to help him dig – but all to no avail.

Keith Harker had been back digging by the triangular stone by 8am that morning, and had been rewarded with three more gold coins. Two of these were dated 1724 and 1725 – both Portuguese. The third coin was a Spanish gold cob type coin that was undated. The British Museum claimed later that this was a forgery of Spanish origin, because the arms were the wrong way around. Later in the year, after the cove had been extensively dug, Keith found another Portuguese 4000 reis coin, dated 1715. This find proved amusing because whilst he was digging the hole, a walker asked him what he was looking for, and he answered, 'Gold coins,' – just as he threw out a shovel full of shingle, from which he picked up a gold coin and remarked, 'Like this one!' The walker was astounded, I believe. Keith's father, Robin, found a solid silver torque bracelet, with snake's head terminals. When found it was inside a lump of concretion and had to be carefully removed. It was later said to be Indian in origin, but I believe Robin is not so convinced. I have seen it and can't make up my mind either way. He also found a 1912 half sovereign in the cove. However, I am not sure exactly when these items were found.

Brian Bradshaw had started digging near the cliff face, nearer to the wall, and to the left of the crevice. He found a 1720 Portuguese 4000 reis, and a 1722 400 reis (one tenth size), and at a later date a brass 1.5 reis dated 1699. The latter coin was found 1m deep in 1981 whilst digging another hole with me (Brian was a regular digger in the cove, and a good friend of mine). He also found a Spanish 2 reals (piece of 2), dated 1782, the date of which turned out to be quite important later. It was very corroded and almost broken in two, but most importantly the date could be clearly seen.

That day I found a French demi em of Louis XIV later dated as 1683 and minted at Rennes. It is about the size of an old half crown, and was very corroded – hence the late identification. I also found 3 musket balls (see map location B and C on page 19) Various other people also found unused lead shot and some concreted copper sheathing complete with half inch copper nails. Altogether about 1000 other modern coins were found at the time, and I know of at least two other people who found (at various times) similar large numbers of modern coins dating from the Victorian period.

Ron and Derek were digging very near me, at a place where I had suggested that coins were possibly still to be found, because, at that time, I believed this to be the case. Thus they worked away in their allotted (claim) area, but never found any gold coins. However, they did find many modern coins which included early Victorian silver, but nothing earlier than this period. They both worked very hard, and toiled all day in vain. This was the true state of affairs that day, with people digging holes all over the place, in what I can only describe as frenzied digging. Various people tended to move from

23

place to place in the hope of finding richer pickings, but luck was against most of them.

Brian Forrest found a square brass coin weight in the cove. It was about 10mm diameter , and 3mm thick, and had stamped on it what looked like a small daisy, with a '-Wi' or something very similar.

I also saw a hammered coin that was found by Nick Pugsley of Ilfracombe. Although the date of the find is not clear, it was a Charles I (1625-49) half-crown, in a worn condition which was found in the cove in the shingle area below the rocks I call the horn, which jut out below the steps on the far side. I was shown this coin when I gave a talk about the wreck of *The London* at a later date in Ilfracombe Museum. The general area where it was found is marked 'A' on the map (see page 19). Apparently it was one of two hammered coins that were corroded together. The other coin was separated by a chemistry teacher when a friend of Nick's took it to school. The second coin, which was thought to be an Elizabethan half-crown was extremely badly corroded and was sold soon after so no more details are known. However, I believe that these coins were lost from an older wreck, or lost at an earlier date than *The London*. Nick also found an iron cannon ball that probably weighed about five pounds, it was very corroded .

I have also heard tell of another gold coin, found around this time, but not what type, nor its date. It is difficult to say for sure if any coins remain in the cove, because there are problems in trying to dig the shingle systematically. The first and most obvious problem is the fact that the tide flows in and out twice a day. The other problem is caused by the fresh water which flows from the field above and constantly fills the bottom of any hole you dig, especially in the winter. It is virtually impossible to dig in the summer due to the number of holiday makers that visit the cove. There is also the problem of the gravel and shingle, constantly sliding in around the edge of the hole. However, there is never a problem caused by holes being left open, because providing the tide reaches far enough up the beach, the hole, and spoil heap is automatically filled in and levelled by the incoming tide.

I must confess that, I too, was smitten by gold fever whilst digging in the cove. It was almost impossible not

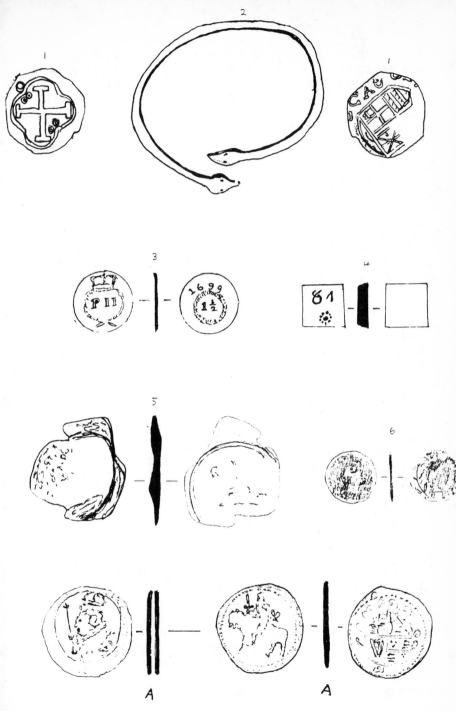

Various finds c.1643-45

to be – especially when the mania reached its height on that Sunday, where the competition for a place to dig was bordering upon the farcical. The atmosphere in the cove that day was so charged that I began to understand the meaning of the words mass hysteria.

The Receiver of wrecks

Well after the excitement of that Sunday gold rush had died down, the receiver of wrecks, Dave Garrett, called down at the cove and spoke to myself and my brother David about the coins found in the cove. He was concerned about the mean high water mark, because it was vital to know if the coins were found within the area which was his responsibility. I remember the day well because it was freezing cold with scattered snow showers flurrying around. I had previously called him to report my coins – which is the correct procedure. A person later asked me why on earth I should bother to report the coins; why I did not just keep them and say nothing. My reply to this was that if I failed to report the coins, I could never tell the story. I'm relieved to say my inner conviction that there *was* a story here – a story that needed to be told – was stronger than any lingering, (though admittedly still powerful) lust for the coins themselves.

Dave Garrett, who was based at Appledore at that time, was trying to encourage people to hand in their gold coins by championing their cause in terms of the best possible reward money. This was reported in the *North Devon Journal Herald*, the local weekly which had previously reported the story of the gold coins found in the cove.

Dave is indeed a very considerate man and was deeply sincere in his wish to preserve these coins for posterity and ultimately he had to abide by the 1894 *Merchant Shipping Act*, which basically states that the finders should receive as much as 75% of their current value – or as little as 25%. The lower percentage was the amount Dave was suggesting the finders could pay (and thus keep their coins) in order to encourage people to hand them in. The finders then had to wait a year and a day, which is the legal amount of time allowed for any claimants to put forward a case for ownership – which no one did. The finders were then offered the coins at the 25% rate of the current value, which was assessed by a reputable dealer – in this case W.H. Lane of Penzance. If the finders declined to buy their coins and chose to sell them for the reward money, the coins were put up for auction, as indeed, some were. Only three of the gold coins were sold, the people who found them receiving 75% of the sale price.

Other Digging Expeditions in Rapparee Cove

In January 1978 Ron Mackie, a colleague and friend of mine, called at my home after seeing the report of the finds in the *North Devon Journal Herald*. He and John Lakeman were keen to arrange to accompany me on a dig, and the following evening after work Ron called around to pick me up in his van.

It was quite dark as we travelled from Barnstaple to Viveham cottage, where John lived with his wife Janet (Jenet). It was bitterly cold and John, replete in a thick woollen hat, was ready to go. He greeted me full of the excitement of being a gold prospector, and began asking me questions about the coins, and the possibility of any more being buried in the cove. Nothing, I believe, at that time that I could have said to him would have have convinced him of anything other than the fact that there were more coins to be found.

The quizzing, and the talking continued until we arrived at Rapparee Cove car-park. We then unloaded the digging gear and two oil lamps, and proceeded along the winding path to the cove. It was an exceptionally dark night, with no reflection off low clouds, and Ron began to get spooked – and having second thoughts – as he considered the conflicting stories I had told him about bodies being drowned with iron fetters still on their legs, and skulls washed up in the cove. Ron was superstitious at the best of times and the cove can be an eerie place after dark – no place for the faint hearted, especially when your shadows start dancing around in the lamp light.

The excitement of searching for the gold soon helped Ron to think positively as we continued down the steep steps and onto the shingle. The tide was quite far out, so we lit the lamps and started to dig further down the beach, to see if anything might still be buried there. By this time our eerie thoughts had completely disappeared, and we were fully concentrated on our search. We dug a trench about 2 metres wide, and just over half a metre deep, in the lower central section of the cove. The frost was biting cold and we managed only to keep warm by working very hard indeed. The trench was finally dug right up to the cliff face after many hours work which had involved moving large rocks with a large iron bar, and eventually we were completely exhausted. By this time we had only found modern coins and a few lead musket balls, so we moved further to the right, where we found two silver Victorian coins and two more musket balls — by now Ron and I were very tired and disheartened, but John was absolutely convinced that a box full of coins lay buried somewhere in the cove; or that the bulk of the coins had gone into the adjoining cove. Ron was just as convinced that luck was against us and after much discussion — heightened by our being extra tired, and confused by heads giddy with paraffin fumes — we gave up the search and headed for home.

After reaching the cottage at Viveham John kept the discussion going for a further two hours — gold fever had got to him — cherishing the idea of finding more buried gold coins. Finally Ron and I, giving way to exhaustion insisted on continuing our journey home.

§

For weeks to come the gold fever was burning deep in the hearts of John and Ron. Although I appeared more sceptical, I never really gave up the prospect of finding the odd gold coin here or there.

The Gold and Other Coins Found in Rapparee Cove

In date order of find

No.	Metal	Description	Date	key to map
1	Silver	Demi em. Louis XIV, French.	1683.	4
2	Gold	Guinea, James 2nd, British.	1686.	1
3	Gold	Moidore, 4000 reis. Peter II Colonial Portug.	1689	2
4	Copper	1.5 reis. Portuguese.	1699	11
5	Gold	Moidore, 4000 reis. Colonial Portuguese.	1715	10
6	Gold	Moidore 4000 reis. Joannes V Colonial Portug.	1720	3
7	Gold	400 reis. Joannes V Colonial Portuguese	1720	6
8	Gold	Moidore 4000 reis. Joannes V Colonial Portug.	1723	8
9	Gold	Portuguese 8 escudo. Joannes V	1723	9
10	Gold	Moidore 4000 reis. Joannes V Colonial Portug.	1724	5
11	Gold	2 escudo/Doubloon, Spanish Colonial.	——	7
12	Gold	Portuguese 8 escudo. Joannes V	1725	12
13	Silver	2 reals. Spanish	1784	13

There are various books and articles that cover the topic of foreign coinage, their weights and their values. The following details have emerged from them. See *Coin Weights fore Gold Coins*, 1987, Chris Marshal.

The Moeda da Ouro, 'Money of Gold'

The Moidore was also known as the four cruzado piece. The cross of Jerusalem was on the reverse and the crowned arms of Portugal on the obverse.

The Moidore or 4000 reis coin was struck in vast quantities from 1663-1720. The Portuguese Brazilian colony issued even larger quantities of these coins, especially after the discovery of gold deposits there. It was the most commonly traded coin in the New World, and the main international gold coin of the 18th century. Some of the four cruzado pieces found at Rapparee cove display the Bs and Rs on the reverse between angles of the cross. The Bs and Rs represent the mints of Bahia and Rio, in Brazil.

The Joannes Piece, or Escudo

In 1722, John V introduced a new coinage based on the gold Escudo. The royal bust and title are on the obverse, and the crowned arms of Portugal are within a decorative shield on the reverse. A popular name for these portrait pieces was 'Joeys,' with was taken from the royal title on the coins. The decorative shield was changed from year to year. See Chris Marshal, 1987. and T. Sheppard and J. F. Musham, 1923, who list various examples.

One Port piece   Eight escudo.   18dwt 10gr.   3 12s 0d

The Portuguese Moidore

One Moidore.   4000 reis.   6dwt 22.25 gr.   1 7s 0d.

The Two Escudo, or Doubloon

This undated Spanish-Mexican coin was minted after 1567, when the double escudo was first introduced, and was also known as a doubloon, or one Pistol. The English value was 17s. There has been a suggestion that this coin was made from Inca gold.

The 1686, James II Gold Guinea

The gold that this coin is made of was originally brought back from Guinea on the west coast of Africa, by the *African Company* and hence the coins that were made from this gold took the name 'Guineas'. The one found in Rapparee Cove was milled in a screw press machine, and had a fixed weight of 129.5 grains, but apparently the actual value fluctuated up until 1717 when it stabilised at twenty shillings.

4

We're Bound to Perish

The gold coins from Rapparee Cove at last gave me some actual evidence. I believed this evidence would give me the vital clue which would lead once and for all to the wreck's name. Nothing could have been further from the truth — this story was never going to be that simple.

I could, however, use the coins to find out numismatic details. I had been convinced for a long time that the wreck had been one of the prizes of Lord Rodney as suggested by the words on a water-colour by Walters in Ilfracombe Museum (see page 62 where it is quoted in full). I persuaded Brian Bradshaw to find and show me the badly corroded French quarter dollar he had found in the cove, and with great difficulty and much perseverance, I managed to make out the date as 1784. I knew by this time that the engagement involving Lord Rodney was in 1782, so clearly the coin could not have come from any of these ships. Thus I had to find more information.

In 1982 I was fortunate enough to be in the Guildhall in Barnstaple, in connection with the *North Devon Rescue Archaeology Committee*, when I met Joy Slocombe. This was when I was first told of an account regarding the wreck of *The London*, which Joy had seen in the records section of Ilfracombe Museum, where she worked. This excited me and I made immediate arrangements to visit the museum.

On arrival I was warmly welcomed by Joy and by John Longhurst. John agreed that there was an existing newspaper extract concerning the wreck of *The London* and given time he would be happy to trace the article and let me have a copy.

He then sent me a letter dated 7th December 1982; the letter stated :

As promised, enclosed is a copy of the account of the wreck of "The London" which we hope may be of interest to you. Do come in and see us again when you are in Ilfracombe.

The account he sent me was from the *Ilfracombe Parish Magazine*, and dated October 1904, which can still be read in Ilfracombe Museum. The report was headed, "The Wreck of *The London*." The article concerned much earlier letters that had appeared in the *Illustrated London News* of 1856. The first of these letters which concern Rapparee Cove was signed by somebody mysteriously calling themselves 'V'. It is worth quoting in its entirety as it undoubtedly set off a chain of events which I believe prove beyond reasonable doubt that the ship which foundered upon the rocks of Rapparee Cove was *The London*:

January 19th 1856

A DEVONSHIRE CUSTOM.— Four and a half miles from Comb-martin is a cove called "The Rapparee (Irish rebel), Cove." Against the cliff, at the north-east angle of this cove, just out of the reach of the flood tides and scarcely below the surface of the earth, are an immense number of human bones, the bodies appearing to been thrown there indiscriminately, not buried. Is it possible that when O'Donnell the Red, Chief of Tirconnell, and son-in-law to the rebel Earl of Tyrone, fled from Ireland (1602), he, or some of his followers, instead of reaching Spain, landed at this cove? and that many of them being here killed, others concealed themselves and were hunted by the country people in the woods between Berrynarbour and Combmartin! If such an event took place it must have been in the time of the Devon historians, Pole, Risdon, and Westcote— the last of whom possessed by marriage property in Combmartin and Berrynarbour. They do not, however, even mention the custom spoken of by HSP. In what year was it discontinued?—V.

The custom to which 'V' is referring is a rather

macabre annual event which is held at nearby Combe Martin to celebrate the legendary hunting of the Irish rebels, as 'V' states. However, it is speculative in the extreme to try and link the remains found in Rapparee Cove to these 'Irish rebels'.

The speculative nature of 'V's letter provoked a scathing response from somebody signing themselves 'N.V.', the contents of whose letter borders upon the libellous. The good people of Ilfracombe will be outraged even today at the nature of his suggestions. I quote in full:

(1856)

THE RAPPAREE COVE.— *In answer to your correspondent "V." it is well known by many old men now living that about sixty years ago a vessel, manned by blacks, ran ashore, and that the then best families in the town (being nothing but wreckers and smugglers) murdered the crew and buried the bodies on the beach, and then plundered the vessel of a very valuable cargo, consisting of ivory, doubloons, jewels, &c. This having caused some disturbance, put an end to the system; otherwise, in bad weather, a common custom was to affix lanterns to horses' tails, and lead them about the cliffs, to decoy vessels. Many near descendants of the actual wreckers of the before-named vessel still reside here, and rank amongst the most respectable of the inhabitants. The people here still retain the name of "Combe Sharks," which appellation was bestowed upon them by the surrounding neighbourhood about a century ago.—N.V., Ilfracombe.*

The Ilfracombe Parish Magazine in October 1904 reporting these letters, is surprising in its frankness:

....There is, unhappily, no doubt whatever that this neighbourhood was guilty in those days, even in the first half of the nineteenth century, of the horrible practice of wrecking, and there was a strong tradition that the fate of 'The London' was not entirely due to the wind and the waves.

However, in 1856 N.V.'s suggestion that the good people of Ilfracombe could be involved in such a foul practice as wrecking provoked the correspondent of the *North Devon Journal* to write on 28th February 1856:

Before calling in the evidence of the 'many old men now living' who the wicked wretch who wrote the paragraph says are well acquainted with the slanderous tale, we may express some surprise at the stupidity, carelessness or worse, of the editor of a paper hitherto thought to be respectable, who could admit into his column such manifest lies and glaring absurdities as are contained in that paragraph.

The first witness we shall call is the 'Annual Register' for the year 1796, the year in which the dreadful wreck occurred.

Under date of October 16th we find this entry :

"This evening a very melancholy accident occurred at Ilfracombe. A ship, called 'The London', from S. Kitts, having on board a considerable number of blacks (French Prisoners) was driven on the rocks near the entrance of the pier during a violent gale of wind, by which about 50 of the prisoners were drowned. Those who got on shore exhibited a most wretched spectacle, and the scene altogether was too shocking for description. The wind was blowing directly fair for the harbour."

Given the serious nature of the charges laid by 'N.V.' the *North Devon Journal* Correspondent was right to publish this account from the *Annual Register*. Still, the *Ilfracombe Parish Magazine* of 1904 seemed surprisingly intent on playing the Devil's Advocate :

We have reason to believe that the wreck took place on October 9th, and not on October 16th.....

....and in the Burial register for October 13th we find that there were two men buried in our churchyard whose names seem to indicate that they may have perished on this occasion.

There were indeed two burials on October 13th 1796 at Holy Trinity Church, Ilfracombe and the names of the two men buried were James Crompton and William Nurenburg. The surname of the latter is admittedly somewhat unusual but is not proof that these men were from *The London*. I subsequently, however, did establish (see page 121) that the wreck *had* taken place on 9th October, and not on the 14th.

Another version of the wreck of *The London* is recorded in a frail, green covered book which Joy Slocombe found for me in the museum, in 1982. This book is grandly titled: *Old Times in the Westcountry: Stories Legends and Highwaymen. Series No 1* and is actually composed of a collection of cuttings from *The Ilfracombe Parish Magazine* – a fact that Jeanne Hardwick later discovered. A few years later I needed to relocate this book in order to help justify my simple (it seemed to me) assertion that the wreck from which the remains at Rapparee had come was *The London*.

That the book was green was the only clue I had about its identity; I knew it was somewhere located in Ilfracombe Museum and I again enlisted the help of the staff. I had subsequently come under so much pressure from the media and other bodies urging me to produce copies of the records I had referred to, that the idea of my not being able to find the Green Book filled me with horror.

We were all searching frantically high and low for the vanished book when it was suddenly spotted tucked away in the archive section, covered in plastic to protect it. There was an audible sigh of relief — at last we had it in our hands again — Thank God!

Here is the account quoted in full from the Green Book:

> *It was late in the evening when a gun was heard faintly booming in the distance. A fine vessel was seen in distress. Who fired the gun is a question I cannot answer, but it was thought most probable it was one of the crew, for the master of the vessel wanted no assistance as it turned out. Finding that he was in a position from which he could not extricate himself, it was supposed that he had determined to die rather than let it be known that he was trading with human freight; that his vessel was loaded with fellow beings as slaves. An Ilfracombe pilot bravely ventured out in response to the signal, but was not allowed to board her. "Where are you from?" demanded the pilot. "From hell bound for damnation," was the awful answer given by the ruffian captain, who had on board such invaluable treasure- a cargo of human life with gold*

and specie, the worth of which none shall ever answer. "Pilot away" exclaimed the captain, "We want no assistance, we're bound to perish," and soon the assertion was realised, and the noble vessel sank beneath the gurgling waters, amidst the agonising cries and shrieks of those on board, thus ruthlessly and desperately deprived of precious life. In the morning the beach was covered with the bodies of the unfortunate Negroes, washed up by the tide; and amongst them, a strange and pitiful exception, like a pearl amongst Rubies, was a lovely creature, a youthful lady. A naked lily fair, lying dead, and cold. Whether it was the body of a captive, or the captain's wife, none could ever tell, but the sea had made no distinction between the white and black victims.

As the waves moved the sand on the beach, heaps of shining coins in gold met the sight of the astonished inhabitants, who were busily removing the dead bodies to the out-houses of the Britannia Hotel. The sight was a wondrous and not unwelcome one. Eagerly they rushed to the treasure. The cry was raised by someone, "Stop, first bury the dead." They hesitated, but the inward voice of conscience re-echoed the mandate, and they returned to their work, and the bodies were hastily buried in the hillside, this being the most convenient spot near at hand, there to rest until the resurrection morn. Whether the gold was got afterwards I don't recollect; but I daresay a good deal was secured.

§

The correspondent of the *North Devon Journal* 28th February did not quote the above report but cited John Chiswell, an Ilfracombe pilot, as his chief witness. He described him, at the time of the interview, as being between eighty and ninety years of age:

....He was then [at the time of the wreck] a young man, engaged as a pilot. Four vessels entered the channel, he tells us, of which this unfortunate ship was one of them, and had just returned to his house at night, when the alarm was raised that a ship was on shore at Rapparee. The ship, it appears, was about

*600 tons burden. She came into the back of the pier,
but, the means of securing her to the buoy failing, she
drifted in the storm on to the Rapparee rocks and
there perished.*

My conclusions by this time, were that the ship as well
as carrying a valuable cargo of coins was also carrying
prisoners — or slaves. Incredibly, as I look back now I
realise that the question whether the dead bodies buried
at Rapparee were slaves or prisoners-of-war did not
really occur to me. I was very interested where the ship
had sailed from and to where it was bound; and its
name; and the circumstances leading to its foundering
upon the rocks. But whether the people locked below
decks were prisoners or slaves seemed secondary. How
naive of me! To the ensuing media circus it was an all
consuming question; and I fully realise now that to the
descendants of the African Nation it is of paramount
importance. Ilfracombe was not ready for this, although
it may well have been due.

The letter in the *Illustrated London News* of January
19th 1856 suggesting that *The London* may have met its
unfortunate end in circumstances which did not reflect
well on the population of Ilfracombe, was signed by 'N.V.'
either because it was – or because it was deliberately
purporting to be – penned by a Nathaniel Vye. It is
interesting that the correspondent of the *North Devon
Journal* following his interview with John Chiswell in his
article of February 28th 1856 goes on to claim that:

> ...*Many of the coloured people on board, as well as
> others, were saved, and for them a shelter was speed-
> ily found in a large stable near the quay, which was
> fitted up, as well as circumstances would allow, for
> their comfort. There were some lady and gentlemen
> passengers who were taken and provided for by Mr
> Lee, father of the late Nathaniel Vye Lee Esq. The
> number of coloured prisoners in the hold of the vessel
> is considered by this witness to have been about sixty.
> It was impossible to get at them, and they were all, as
> stated in the Register, drowned in the wreck. Many
> others also perished, and, as they were washed in,
> not all at once, their bodies were buried deep in the
> sand.*

The Pilot John Chiswell

Further details concerning John Chiswell seemed to me to be worth searching for and the following were uncovered, largely due to the work of Jeanne Hardwick in preparation for a later documentary by HTV.

John Chiswell was baptised in Ilfracombe on August 1st 1773. He was 23 years old when the wreck of *The London* took place in 1796. He was living in High Street, Ilfracombe when the 1851 census was taken, which gave the following details:

High Street
Martha Prescot, widow 79, head, born Braunton.

Maria Prescot, daughter, 45 unmarried, retired servant, born Ilfracombe.

John Chiswell, head, married aged 77, born Ilfracombe (1773). Proprietor of houses.

Elizabeth Chiswell, wife, aged 73 . Born Ilfracombe.

Hannah Chiswell, daughter, unmarried aged 42 dress maker. Born Ilfracombe.

Mary Chiswell, daughter, unmarried, aged 38, dress maker. Born Ilfracombe.

Samuel Chiswell, son, unmarried, aged 33, tailor journeyman. Born Ilfracombe.

John Chiswell is next mentioned in an extract in the Green book in Ilfracombe Museum. The book is called *Old Times in the Westcountry; Stories Legends, Traditions and Rhymes of Old North Devon, Part 1*. This account may have been written or compiled in 1873. In this book the author tells us that John Chiswell's father was drowned within sight of Ilfracombe.

A tombstone can be seen in Ilfracombe Parish Church cemetery. The stone is in very good condition, with no obvious weathering. However, there is a crack on one side of it and it leans forward slightly. The following lines are recorded on it:

In memory of John Phillips Chiswell who died
February 22 1862, aged 88yrs,
also Elizabeth, wife of the above died
June 29 1870, aged 93 yrs,
also Hannah Keall Chiswell
daughter of the above John and Elizabeth Chiswell
died September 22 1882 aged 73 yrs,
also Mary Chiswell daughter of the above died
June 16 1890 aged 80 yrs.

A card with these details can be found in Ilfracombe Museum, and is numbered 239 gg, H/S. The 'gg' written on this card, stands for 'girl guides,' which represents the area where the stone can be seen in the cemetery. Jeanne, who is deeply involved in Genealogy has spent a long time recording the gravestones of Ilfracombe Parish Church Cemetery, and is happy to help people with their family history. Jeanne compiled the following details of the Chiswell family tree:

Thomas Chiswell was from Woolwich.
He was buried on 22nd April 1750 , aged 71 years.

John Chiswell married Elizabeth (Phillips?)
He was born in 1736 and was buried in 1819.

John Chiswell born and died in 1770
Thomas Chiswell was baptised in 1778
John Phillips Chiswell baptised in 1773 married Elizabeth Keall

The children of **John Phillips Chiswell** and Elizabeth Keall were:

John	Thomas	Elizabeth	Hannah Keall	Mary
b.1798	b.1801	b.1803	1806–82	1809-90

William Keall	Joseph	Samuel	James	
b.1811	b.1814	1817–1908	b.1820	

Thomas (b.1801) married Mary Dyer in 1827.
Their children were Thomas 1828-49 and John Phillips 1836-63.

Samuel (b.1817) married Charlotte (?) who was buried in 1915.

5

Remains at Rapparee

In the meantime Joy had written to the National Maritime Museum in London and sent me a copy of their answer regarding the wreck of *The London*, in a letter dated 22nd April 1985, Mr C J Ware from the Readers' Services Section, wrote:

I have found the following reference to the loss of 'The London' in Lloyd's List:

"Friday 14th October 1796: 'The London', transport; Robertson, from St Lucia is Lost near Ilfracombe."

From this it would appear that the master was Robertson. In Lloyd's Register there is a LONDON, built at Shoreham 1764, 300 tons, owner S Mather, with a master of that name. She appears in the register for '95 but is gone in '96 making it a strong possibility that this is your LONDON. As a transport she would have been hired by the Admiralty from the owner for the voyage. The West Indies were heavily disputed at the time, most likely that she was a troop transport on a return voyage.

A more recent letter dated 6th March 1997 was sent to me from Nigel Rigby at the National Maritime Museum, London, after he had visited my home. The letter reads as follows:

She was apparently registered as a ship – which is to say a three masted vessel, fully square rigged on all three masts – of 300 tons. A barque also could have three masts, but the aftermost mast would have been fore and aft rigged. My memory is that it was a little hard to tell from the painting how she was rigged. 'The

London' had been thoroughly refitted in 1788, had a new deck put in in 1789, and is described in Lloyd's Register as being in good condition in 1795. Fully loaded she drew 15ft. Whilst I've found the entry describing her loss – which Chris Ware sent you – I've not been able to trace any record of her movements in the year before she was wrecked. There are several 'Londons' mentioned in Lloyds List (which records the actual movement of shipping from week to week) toddling around the Caribbean that year, but none appear to be the 'right' one. According to Lloyd's Register for 1793, 1794. and 1795 her destination for each year was Honduras, which sounds as though she had a regular shuttle service across the Atlantic. I'm told that if she had been hired as a transport by the Admiralty for any of those years it should show up in this particular column, so as she does not it seems probable that she was hired in the West Indies especially to transport the bullion and prisoners back to England.

The story of The London had begun to emerge at last, but many people were still unconvinced, even, that I had the right ship. One problem seemed to be my adamant belief in the accuracy of old records. I had no reason to doubt these accounts – however varied in degrees they may be. Of course it is possible that the original writers really believed in their records – but that such records were actually mistaken. For example, what if the bodies were buried in the north east angle of the cove from the wreck of The London, but in the process of such burial, disturbed earlier burials – those speculatively suggested by 'V' in the 1856 account as being from Ireland being a case in point. Both reports could be correct. There may have been bodies already buried in this location from various periods — as it happens it is the only earthy area in the cove. Scientific bone analysis may eventually reveal this to be the case. However, to my knowledge there has never been another wreck mentioned which suggests that large amounts of gold coins were on board.

§

40

In 1991, by which time I was now living in Ilfracombe, Alison Mills (deputy museums manager and curator of the Museum of North Devon) rang to ask if I would be prepared to loan the coins I had found for a display in the small St Anne's Chapel Museum in the Parish Church Barnstaple, to which I readily agreed. The display featured an enlarged photograph of the water colour by Walter depicting the wreck of *The London*.

The captions below the displays told the story of my researches and my discoveries up until that time and Alison asked me if I would be good enough to let the *North Devon Journal* take a picture of me digging in the cove.

While posing – spade in hand – for the *Journal* photograph I noticed that the wall in the north east angle of the cove had been partly demolished by recent storms and it struck me that there could be bones protruding from the eroded bank just behind. An inspection was made and although the erosion at that time was back to a depth of one metre no bones were showing. This was the first time it had occurred to me to *actually look* for bones, although when I had drawn a map of the cove back in 1978 showing the location of the coins, I had boldly written: 'SITE OF BONES'. I was fortunate, also, to have taken a picture of the bank and wall in 1984 because interestingly this photograph shows a small section of wall on the cliff crevice where later (in February 1997) ironwork was found by which time this section of wall was completely gone. This ironwork which was concreted to the rock by the chemical action of the sea, can therefore only have become exposed between 1984 and 1991 (a fuller explanation of the significance of the ironwork appears later)

§

A further related sequence of events began with a telephone call in 1997 whilst I was analysing medieval pottery from Duckpool farm at Mortehoe – a site some five miles down the coast from Rapparee and one I had been excavating since 1996. Following this telephone call my life would never be the same again.

It was the morning of February 17th and the call was from Jeanne Hardwick at Ilfracombe Museum. She told me that Peter Russell had found some bones in

Rapparee. I had so familiarised myself by this time with the history of the cove, that I had little need to ask her the location of the find.

Quietly I stated, "That's the location where the 1856 account mentions that a huge number of bones were buried in the north east angle of the cove."

Jeanne later affirmed that Allison Mills had recommended to Ilfracombe Museum, that they contact me on the matter. Then Joy Slocombe invited me to call down to the museum where I was shown a plastic bag containing fragments of human bones which Jeanne had collected by scratching through the spoil left by Peter. There were twenty fragments in this bag containing various bones, and I recognised one in particular as an eye socket. Jeanne told me how difficult her task had been, trying not to attract the attention of people wandering around the beach. She then again described the location at the north east angle of the cove, which is at the top of the beach under the cliffs.

I hurried to visit the site, to record and retrieve anything that was left. My first view into the cove from the high steps that drop steeply down showed that the sloping bank – in the north east angle towards the arched stone shelter – was deeply eroded behind what remained of the stone ditched wall.

I then went over to the remnant of the wall on the far side of the cove to see just how much erosion had been caused behind the wall by recent storms. I knew that the wall had been first breached in 1991, and now I could compare a recent photograph with the two earlier ones. It had been eroded back from 1 metre in 1991, to 2.5 metres now. The deepest part of the eroded bank was about 5 metres at the top in the central position.

On closer examination I noticed a small amount of spoil at the foot of the eroded bank behind the old wall, and scratched through it, picking up another thirty three bone fragments (mostly skull) some of which were washed clean by the heavy rain that was now falling. From the foot of the collapsed bank to the stone ditching in the wall is a distance of 2.5 metres and here I spotted another bone in a portion of stable earth.

I carefully scratched the face of the slope at this point and to the left below a band of clay. Three articulated finger bones were now clear to see – about 4.8

metres from where the stone ditching abutted the cliff rock, on the right of the site. Two of these bones fell out, as the earth crumbled and I managed to recover these and kept them together covered with a round flat stone. I was sure that there were more bones from this articulated group, so finding another flat stone, I placed this over the remaining spoil, which I resolved to sieve when the site was excavated.

On the way back home, I called in at the museum and Joy tried to arrange permission from Ilfracombe town council to dig the site. She was told that permission had to be obtained from North Devon District Council. Jeanne rang them and was referred to John Parkinson, who gave verbal permission — and when asked if we needed permission in writing he answered, "No, my word is enough."

I began making arrangements for the rescue dig to take place on Saturday 22nd February 1997, before any remaining fragments were washed away by the high tides which I knew were due the following week.

In the meantime the police had called at the museum and taken away the bones Peter Russell had found, thinking they may be evidence for a murder inquiry. I had to visit the police station the next morning and bring them up to date concerning all the information I had uncovered concerning the bones at Rapparee Cove. The Sergeant was at Lynton that day, so the duty officer said he would have him ring me later.

The coroner Mr James had been trying to telephone me and when I returned his call he told me that the bones had gone up to the Pathology Laboratory, at the North Devon District Hospital, and were deemed to be of an age which rendered them of no interest to the police. Mr James had sat mesmerised as I related to him the story of the bones at Rapparee as it had so far unfolded – I was excited by the knowledge that I was safe to go ahead with the excavation on Saturday. .

Events were now hotting up apace and back home I received a call from Joy at the museum to say that Linda Blanchard of North Devon District Council wanted to speak to me about the bones. I arranged to meet her at the harbour car park near the cove and from here we walked down into Rapparee, where I showed her the site and explained the details of the finds. When we looked at the actual location on the beach, I immediately noticed that it had been disturbed, and an iron bar had been left upright beside a newly collapsed pile of soil and shale from above. I could not relocate the finger bones in the lower bank, since the disturbance had covered my protecting marker stones (these later turned out to be exactly where the point of the iron bar was buried).

We left the site and returned to the car and discussed the bones. Linda was satisfied that the bones were human and agreed to help in any way possible. She offered me some surplus equipment from the disbanded Barnstaple Archaeological Unit, and some personal garden equipment suitable for digging. I agreed that I would be glad to take the equipment which was stored at her house at Barbrook. Linda then asked me if I thought that a little publicity might be of use, and when I agreed she offered to contact a journalist that lives near her – the reporter Nick Constable – and ask him to visit the cove on Saturday bringing the equipment along with him. Linda also expressed a wish to be involved herself on the Saturday but it was clearly dangerous for her children – who she would not be able to supervise while concentrating on digging.

§

By the Wednesday evening I had arranged with various people to meet for the dig on Saturday, they included : Margaret Reed and Rosemary Akers; Jeanne's husband George, and (of course) my wife Rosamund. Alison Mills said she would try to get over if possible. Later in the week Richard Ashford rang me to confirm that he would be over to help.

On the 18th February, Sergeant Harrison telephoned me to ask what would happen to the bones when I picked them up from Ilfracombe police station. I told him that Ilfracombe Museum intended to hold on to them, which he thought was a very good idea. He also told me that he had met Peter Russell in the evening at Rapparee — after I had visited the cove — and that Peter had noticed the two round stones which showed that someone else had been there. This explained the iron bar left beside the newly collapsed pile of shale. I ended the confusion by confessing to Sergeant Harrison that the 'someone else' had been me!

44

By 3pm on 19th February the police had rung back to say that the bones had arrived from the coroner's office and I could pick them up, which I did about 4.15pm. There were 15 bones in a brown A4 size envelope, which included 2 teeth and some skull fragments, a piece of jawbone and an arm radius bone fragment.

Peter had found 15 fragments prior to 17th February, which were handed in to Ilfracombe Museum. Later these were passed back to me from the coroner. Jeanne found another 20 fragments after she reinvestigated the spoil, and I found a further 35 in the same spoil after that. This now made a total of 70 bone fragments before the main dig was started.

Fragments of Bones Identified prior to 22nd Feb. 1997

21 cranial fragments	2 teeth	1 left jawbone.
2 metacarpals	1 vertebra	1 carpal.
2 phalanxes		1 eye socket.
4 vertebra frags.		

§

Rosamund and I were ready to leave for the cove by five minutes past eight, Richard Ashford had not arrived by eight o'clock so we drove the car over to the car-park by the new sewerage works, and unloaded our digging equipment. It took me two trips loaded with equipment to get it all down into the cove, Roz watching the car while I was gone. On the second trip back up to the car I saw Richard arriving by the harbour entrance, and I waited to give him directions to the cove. I called out to where he stood by the wall and he eventually heard me.

Back in the cove Roz had gone on and moved most of the equipment into the shelter and we started to put the tools and measuring equipment by the eroded bank, behind the fallen stone ditched wall. In the meantime, George arrived. He immediately helped me to take measurements at the site, whilst Richard tidied up the collapsed pile of soil and shale left following Sergeant Harrison's visit with Peter. Richard then piled loose debris behind the remaining stone ditched retaining wall, in order to support and back it up. Next he flattened off a platform on top of the freshly piled heap behind the wall. I then asked him to investigate the bank behind the heap, where he found some human bones – rib fragments and a hand carpal bone but nothing else of consequence.

I had originally taken measurements on 17th February of the location where the skull fragments and finger bones were seen that were in an articulate position (possibly connected to the lower arm bones No. 1), and these enabled me to find the exact location again immediately. The iron bar which the police had used to investigate the site on the evening of 17th February was still sticking in the shingle and mud slippage.

In the meantime Margaret Reed had arrived in Ilfracombe and was asked directions to the cove by a newspaper photographer from Chudleigh, Richard Lappas, who was waiting to meet Nick Constable, the National news reporter. Luckily, I spotted Margaret and Richard half-way across Larkstone Beach, heading in the wrong direction and after attracting their attention they accompanied me down into the cove. Nick then arrived and we discussed the progress of my research beginning in the early 1970s.

Then we all moved to a location further down the beach in order to get a better angle for photographs. Nick said he would circulate the story to various national press editions, including *The Times*, and the *Guardian*. Next, a photographer from the *North Devon Journal* appeared, and we shuffled around some more before he thanked us and left. The rest of us went back to the stone shelter by the site, and a copy was taken of my photograph of the painting of the wreck of the London, (the original still hangs in Ilfracombe Museum). Nick was sitting in the stone shelter by a folding table I had brought along for recording drawings on, and had been studying my copies of the old written records while making copious notes. It turned out later that the notes Nick was paying particular attention to, were those which mentioned the slaves — such as those by Mrs Slade-King, in 1879 (see page 12).

I had found Mrs Slade-King's account interesting enough to relate it in an article entitled 'Seeking out the Treasures of History' which appeared in the *North Devon Journal* on 25th July 1991. The publication of this article coincided with the event organised by Alison Mills in St. Anne's Chapel, Barnstaple, where the coins from the wreck which I had lent her were on display.

After Nick had read the account from the Green Book, in Ilfracombe Museum, he asked me a question. Why was it that the captain of the ship (who we now believe to have been called Robertson) declined the assistance offered by the Ilfracombe pilot, John Chiswell? (see page 34). It has to be remembered that at this time the media frenzy which was to descend upon Ilfracombe had not yet occurred. In addition the question as to whether the black people on board were slaves or prisoners-of-war had not appeared, to me, to be the most interesting aspect of the story. The only answer I could offer to Nick's question, bearing in mind that I was also trying desperately to organise the dig at the time, was that the skipper was worried that the local people would discover the slaves in the hold, and try to release them. Nick looked doubtful and, with notebook in hand, stood up and with his photographer, left the cove. With hindsight, I suspect my answer was weak.

We started digging on the site and it soon became apparent that the press had missed the real action shots as bones were being found in numbers.

George, for example, was washing buckets of mud and stone in a sieve, and had dug a small sump in which the water could collect. The flowing water was proving plentiful and Richard enlarged the sump with his long handled shovel, and the pit soon filled. In addition a channel was dug along the collapsed face above where we were digging, thus allowing more water to flow into George's pool, which he used successfully for the rest of the dig. Although the site was extremely wet and muddy the sun shone for us that day.

At some stage Mrs Russell (the mother of Peter) arrived with two little girls and told us how her son had found the bones. She left after a while when one of the little girls protested that she was cold .Then George's wife, Jeanne, arrived with their son Steve, and his little daughter. After showing them my growing collection of files about the wreck, and the three trays of bones which were now displayed, Roz and I decided to return home as we felt that the trays of bones should be stored for safe-keeping.

§

We returned after a short while to discover that Richard had uncovered a radius and ulna bone (group No.1), near a scapula shoulder bone (No.2). These were the first bones to be uncovered in undisturbed shale and clay, other than those exposed by the slight subsidence of the whole slope. These bones may have been cast up over the bank at various times in the past when the retaining wall below was rebuilt. The bones were 23cm long, and their location was 4.5m from the right cliff face, next to the remaining wall, and 2.8m from the face of the stone ditching which had survived the storm (see Illustration opposite).

Richard carefully trowelled the bones clear of shale and clay and washed them off before I took photographs. We also had to be very careful because the loose shale above, and slightly behind these bones, was falling in small amounts all the time. This had to be removed to stop further slippage, which was a constant threat; due to water flowing through the shale of the bank .

Whilst the overburden was being reduced for safety, a pair of humerus arm bones were encountered. These were 3.29m from the front of the remaining wall and 7.30m from the mooring post. The second bone of this pair was broken in several places due to being soft, and with the crushing weight of the overlying shale. The ball joint (No. 7) of bone (No. 4) was found in the bank as the excavation was about to finish.

Several other fragments were uncovered nearby; these were from ribs, various small finger bones, and five skull fragments. The skull fragments were found 0.4m from the original skull fragments found by Peter, Jeanne, and myself. The aspect of human tragedy associated with the finding of these fragments was brought home to us with a vengeance when they were subsequently identified as being from a child, 4-8 years old. I remember it occurring to me at the time how strange that there should have been children aboard the ship – it is unlikely that 6 year olds could be considered prisoners-of-war.

These fragments (No. 6) were 3.05m from the remaining wall face at an angle of 90 degrees. They were also 0.4m above what may have been a shallow grave cutting which contained the two ulna and radius bones (No. 1).

5th April
Rappanee Co-
Pat Barrow [?]

The next bone (No. 5) found was 3.29m from the wall and in front of it, next to the child's skull fragments. This bone may have been the humerus bone of the child. The smallest phalange terminal bone was washed out of the spoil from this area, and may have been from a child's finger bone.

In the meantime various other people had begun arriving at the site. They were Dave Parker and his wife Julie; Rosemary Akers, who was at that time chairman of *North Devon Archaeological Society* incorporating *North Devon Rescue Archaeology*, whom I had invited along. She spoke casually to us before making her apologies and leaving. Last to arrive, just before we stopped digging, was Peter Russell's girlfriend Lesley, and her son. After showing great interest in the site she rushed home to change, wanting to help with the trowelling and actually found terminal upper arm bone (No. 7).

At 3.40pm the distance from the face of the existing wall base had increased from 2.5m to 3.3m. During this time Lesley's son had been looking at something on the concrete steps in front of the wall. He attracted my attention, and in the running water I could see another human tooth. Lesley confirmed that this was the location where Peter and herself had washed off the first bone fragments on Friday 14th February 1997 before taking them down to Ilfracombe Museum. The tooth had been lost, and since that time the mud must have been washed off by the flowing fresh water over the concrete at the foot of the wall.

It was now nearly 5.00pm and Richard announced firmly that he had to go. As he was leaving he passed near a narrow cleft in the rock by the site wall and noticed some corroded ironwork, which looked remarkably like iron fetters. We all rushed over to see them, and immediately agreed with Richard's deduction. There was some doubt cast upon this deduction at a later date – as it seems there was to be doubt cast upon most of our conclusions for reasons which varied depending upon who was casting the doubt. Much of this is discussed in a later chapter.

I filmed the scene on my camcorder, as we found the ironwork, before deciding to return the next day (Sunday) to dig it out. Meanwhile it was getting late so we started to tidy up in preparation for leaving. Dave

Rapparee
Cove
Ilfracombe.

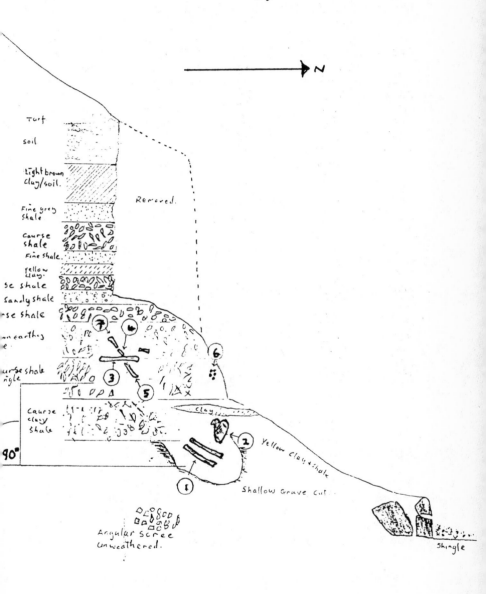

N

Turf

soil

Light brown
clay/soil.

Removed.

Fine grey
shale

Coarse
shale

Fine shale.

Yellow
clay.

se shale

Sandy shale

rse shale

n earthy
e

urse shale
ngle

Caurse
clay
Shale

90°

Clay

Yellow Clay & shale

Shallow Grave Cut

Angular scree
unweathered.

Shingle

Parker and his wife Julie gave us a hand to carry the equipment out of the cove and back to the car. We had all taken the digging very seriously and everyone we spoke to that day was very interested, and extremely friendly. The weather had stayed fine and sunny all day, which had helped to keep us all in good spirits. I thus left the site feeling satisfied — after all, the bones had been found in the location which my research into the records had suggested. In fact, after so many years wondering if the bones would ever be unearthed I felt extremely elated.

§

Returning next day, armed with a lump hammer and cold chisel I began to dislodge the ironwork, which could not have been removed with lesser tools. Roz came with me, and she filmed the event. The so-called fetters had caused great excitement having been referred to in the old records.

Within a week the tide had washed George's spoil heap away, and cleaned off the area where the bones had been found so thoroughly that not even a lose stone remained — only hard packed muddy clay.

The clay below would need to await to be explored — I was convinced that it still held evidence of more burials. Indeed, the upright face of the bank still displayed an interesting stratum, and two of the strata — one at the base, and one about 1.5 metres up, had nodules of lime protruding from them. However, at this time no bones were showing in the stratum, at any level.

Another Receiver of Wrecks

The receiver of wrecks at this time was Mrs Rosemary Skeats who contacted me by telephone whilst I was at Ilfracombe Museum on 28th February 1997. I had to fill out one of their forms entitled 'The Coastguard Agency, Report of Wreck and Salvage' which is basically a finder's report. Once this was completed and returned, Mrs Skeats then sent me back the following reply, dated 10th March 1997:

WELL KNOWN
FACES

TWO LIFEBOATSMEN

Sketches at Ilfracombe from the *Illustrated London News*

Thank you for the completed Report of Wreck form, which is duly recorded.

I note that you do not wish to claim salvage in respect of expenses incurred, and the recovery of these items was carried out on behalf of Ilfracombe Museum.

The receiver of Wrecks is therefore able to offer the items as described by you and listed below, for display at the museum.

200+ Bone fragments.
1 Iron spike 22cm long, 1.5cm wide.
1 Iron nail 19cm long, 1cm wide.
1 Iron tapered flat bar and short length of chain— (fetter?)

I understand that the bone fragments are presently at the museum and would be grateful if you could inform me when transfer of the remaining items has taken place.

The Receiver of Wreck's responsibility for these items is now discharged and Droit no: 447/97 officially closed.

I would thank you for your assistance in this matter.

Yours sincerely

Rosemary Skeats (Mrs).

§

The Site Stratum

As far as could be ascertained all the original layers had sloped down at 45-60 degrees, and the excavated bones found were on a slope at this angle. The remaining underlying layers may reflect this incline if they were to be extensively excavated.

Different colours could be seen in the stratum of the site bank in Rapparee Cove, and were as follows:

Below the turf level was a dark humus layer mixed with natural soil that had built up over the years. Below

A Devonshire Custom.—Four and a half miles from Comb-martin, is a cove called "The Rapparee (Irish rebel) Cove." Against the cliff, at the north-east angle of this cove, just out of the reach of the flood tides, and scarcely below the surface of the earth, are an immense number of human bones, the bodies appearing to been thrown there indiscriminately, not buried. Is it possible that when O'Donnell the Red, Chief of Tirconnell, and son-in-law to the rebel Earl of Tyrone, fled from Ireland (1602), he, or some of his followers, instead of reaching Spain, landed at this cove! and that many of them being here killed, others concealed themselves and were hunted by the country people in the woods between Berrynarbour and Combmartin! If such an event took place it must have been in the time of the Devon historians, Pole, Risdon, and Westcote—the last of whom possessed by marriage property in Combmartin and Berrynarbour. They do not, however, even mention the custom spoken of by H. S. P. In what year was it dis continued!—V.

The Rapparee Cove.—In answer to your correspondent "V.," it is well known to many old men now living that about sixty years ago a vessel, manned by blacks, ran ashore, and that the then best families in the town (being nothing but wreckers and smugglers) murdered the crew and buried the bodies on the beach, and then plundered the vessel of a very valuable cargo, consisting of ivory, doubloons, jewels, &c. This having caused some disturbance, put an end to the system; otherwise, in bad weather, a common custom was to affix lanterns to horses' tails, and lead them about the cliffs, to decoy vessels. Many near descendants of the actual wreckers of the before-named vessel still reside here, and rank amongst the most respectable of the inhabitants. The people here still retain the name of "Coombe Sharks," which appellation was bestowed upon them by the surrounding neighbourhood about a century ago.—N. V., Ilfracombe.

105

F.

THE WRECK OF "THE LONDON."

In the year 1856 some correspondence was published in the *Illustrated London News* concerning various matters relating to North Devon, and the equanimity of the Ilfra-combe correspondent of the *North Devon Journal* was considerably disturbed by a letter which was written about the wreck of *The London* in Rapparee Cove in 1796. There is, unhappily, no doubt whatever that this neigh-bourhood was guilty in those days, and even in the first half of the nineteenth century, of the horrible practice of wrecking, and there was a strong tradition that the fate of *The London* was not entirely due to the winds and waves. We have reason to believe that the wreck took place on October 9th, and not on October 16th, as stated in the fol-lowing account; and in the Burial Register for October 13th we find that two men were buried in our Churchyard whose names seem to indicate that they may have perished on this occasion. The letter published in the *Illustrated London News* was signed "N.V.", the initials being appar-ently chosen to suggest that the writer was Mr. Nathaniel Vye. The letter was as follows:—

"In answer to your correspondent, 'V.', it is well known to many old men now living that about 60 years ago a vessel manned by blacks ran ashore, and that the then best families in the town, being nothing but wreckers and smugglers, murdered the crew and buried the bodies on the beach, and then plundered the vessel of a very valuable cargo, consisting of ivory, doubloons, jewels, etc. This having caused some disturbance put an end to the system; otherwise, in bad weather, a common custom was to affix lanterns to horses' tails, and lead them about the cliffs to decoy vessels. Many near descendants of the actual wreckers of the before-named vessel still reside here, and rank among the most respectable of the inhabitants. The people here still retain the name of *Coombe Sharks*, which appellation was bestowed on them by the surround-ing neighbourhood about a century ago.—N.V., Ilfra-combe."

that a light brown clay and soil mixture was clearly defined. Then a layer of fine grey shale followed by coarse shale, overlaying a fine shale. A yellow clay band followed, overlaying another layer of coarse shale. Then a fine sandy shale lay on top of yet another coarse shale layer, followed by a brown earthy shale. Next came coarse shale mixed with beach shingle, overlaying coarse shale and yellow clay. It is in this yellow clay that the burials may have originated. Clearly the disturbed bones, and articulated remains came from this clay which predates the walls built in this part of the cove.

The building of these walls may have caused the bones in this location to be moved and redistributed an unknown number of times, and the scree that had moved down the slope – or the shale and shingle that was thrown up to cover the bones – occurred after the walls were built; an event which may originally have happened in the mid 19th century, when complaints were being aired concerning the apparent visibility of the bones in this part of the cove. The coarse shale and shingle layer above the bones indicate that the shingle was cast up from the beach level, and was not just scree slipping down from above. However, higher levels may also have been formed in this way at a later date.

Sighting of Bones After 22nd February 1997

A few days after the dig whilst I was talking to some people at a newly erected fence, which effectively closed the cove to the public, three boys came along and one of them told me he had recently found a bone amongst the rocks at the site. When I asked him what he had done with it, he answered, "I put it back again." I examined the site and could see that there was a newly collapsed pile of shale at the foot of the bank. Clearly somebody had been looking for bones .

Skulls noticed in Rapparee Cove Since 1995
From an Interview with Paul Howard
26th February 1997.

Val Ley, a neighbour, stopped Roz and myself in Ilfracombe High Street, and told us that a relative of hers, called Paul Howard had found a jaw-bone in the cove a few years before. It had been sent to the pathology laboratory by the local police, and she believed the laboratory had confirmed that the jawbone was from a Negro. She suggested that I call and ask Paul, since his home was nearby.

That evening at 7pm I knocked on Paul's door, and without hesitation Paul confirmed that just over two years earlier, shortly after he was married, he had seen a skull protruding from the bank where the recent bones had been found. The skull was facing outwards, and the back of the cranium had fallen in. A jaw-bone with two sets of large white teeth was resting about 40cm away. The skull was large and crumbled, because the bone was soft; so he took the jaw and teeth away for the police to examine. After waiting a while, and not hearing from the police, he contacted them again, to ask about the bones. The police informed him that the bones had been examined in the pathology laboratory and were of an age which rendered them of no legal interest. He then asked if they knew where the bones had originated, and the police had replied that the bones were *probably from slaves buried in the bank.*"

Paul often enjoyed walking his dog at Rapparee, and at a more recent date had spotted yet another skull with a long section of spine still attached; he described this one as "coming out of the bank." Since that time, he claimed to have seen another skull — as recently as a week ago; just before the site was brought into the spotlight by press reports. This skull may be the same as that found by Peter Russell.

6

Controversy

In February I contacted Sergeant Harrison to ask him if he knew what had happened to the bones Paul Howard had taken to the police station and he told me that he was not at Ilfracombe station at that time and did not know.

Later (on 2nd August 1997), whilst at a committee meeting regarding erecting a monument in Rapparee Cove, in the presence of North Devon District Council representatives, I was asked by Chairman Bernie Grant MP, to enquire again about what had happened to the bones found by Paul Howard.

I visited Ilfracombe police station on Monday 3rd August, and two officers there told me to contact Keith James at the Coroner's Office, because they did not have any details at that station.

I rang that office at 11-35am the same day. The secretary told me to ring their Barnstaple office and I was put through to Mr James. He told me that he had been in that office for 8 years, but knew nothing about the particular bones in question. I asked him if he knew whether the police were required to keep records of items sent to the Coroner. He told me that it would be unlikely that they could find any such record since the bones had not been booked in. He did suggest, however, that it may be worth enquiring of the Public Records Office in Barnstaple whether they had *any* Coroner's Inquisition papers even dating back as far as 1796.

I rang the local Public Records Office, later that day, and was told that there were no Coroner's Inquisition papers surviving before the Second World War. This was the end of my line of enquiry regarding what happened to the bones given to the police by Paul Howard.

The Ironwork Found in the Cliff Ledge

The ironwork had originally been covered by a wall to the right of the site that could be seen in a photo taken by me in 1984. The wall had subsequently been washed away by storms, leaving the inward sloping ledge exposed for the first time in many years. The ironwork, which is a chain-like structure, was firmly concreted onto the bottom of the crevice, and before it was removed from the crevice, it was noticed that the large end link had been prised open, possibly by using two bars which accompanied it. The remaining metalwork comprised a length of the corroded chain that itself was joined through a hole in the metal bar. Also at this time the other two bars appeared to be an integral part of the whole.

It looked to me to be an iron fetter, minus its clamp section. Once removed from the crevice it could be seen that the fabric of the iron was wrought and was hammered into shape — it has to be conceded that this gave the ironwork a less convincing appearance. The links had been individually made from straight bars that were twisted twice at 90 degree angles from the first loop. Two end links were larger and not twisted, one of which had been prised open, perhaps by the two accompanying bars (which may have been large ship's nails. The links were 3.5mm and 8mm in diameter — the strength of such a chain should not be underestimated. The iron appears to have been deliberately thrown up onto the ledge, and once there it naturally rolled down to the bottom — as did my chisel when I dropped it. I wondered why it would have been thrown there and it came naturally to my mind that whoever prized open the link cast the whole thing onto the ledge in disgust at its grim use — assuming, of course, that it *did have* a grim use.

Nigel Rigby from the *National Maritime Museum* came and inspected the ironwork, and showed me some photos of examples of fetters. I was struck that no two examples

were alike, and as such may have been individually made by various blacksmiths. Thus if the ironwork found in Rapparee Cove does not confirm to pre-conceived ideas of what fetters should look like, it seems to me that this does not rule out the strong possibility that this was the original use. Of course these chains may have been used to fetter prisoners-of-war in the hold of *The London*; it is likely to prove impossible to be sure.

§

The following Monday morning on 24th February 1997, the story that hit the newspapers was like a raging storm. By the end of that day I had been contacted by (among others): *The African Reparation Movement*; *HTV Bristol*; *Radio Bristol*; *County Press Association*; *BBC Plymouth*; *Westcountry TV*; *the BBC in London*; *BBC Bristol*; *Radio 5 Live*; and *the North Devon Gazette & Advertiser*.

I was constantly on the telephone giving interviews, as the interest from the newspapers seemed to take on a momentum of its own. The Monday started at 8.30am with a phone call from a *Radio Four Today* presenter who asked me had I seen the headlines in the *Daily Telegraph*,(which I hadn't) and would I let him interview me live on his programme at 11am (which I did). He asked if I felt the discovery was likely to change my life and this took me back for a moment, because it had never once occurred to me the impact on my family that this was likely to have.

I had not seen any papers so far that day and after the interview Roz and I escaped for a few minutes down to Jeffrey's Newsagents in Ilfracombe where we bought several newspapers in order to try and grasp the scale of the excitement. The *Telegraph* featured Nick Constable's article, and the caption read SHIPWRECK SLAVES GRAVE UNEARTHED. It contained these chilling words:

A mass grave containing the bodies of shipwrecked slaves has been uncovered on a holiday beach.
Up to 60 bodies are thought to lie beneath the cliff of Rapparee Cove near Ilfracombe, North Devon, where the treasure ship 'London' foundered with all hands 200 years ago.

Having read this article I realised that this was the cause of the media frenzy. I had deduced from the records that the negroes who had died on *The London* were either prisoners-of-war or slaves (or both) but the media were not interested in prisoners-of-war, they were only interested in slaves.

The circus continued — film crews wanted pictures of the site in the cove; and *Westcountry TV* used my camcorder footage of the Saturday excavation, as their main news item, and incorporated shots of the painting from Ilfracombe Museum. The painting also featured prominently in the *Daily Telegraph*, and in three other national newspapers. The *Times* read: BEACH YIELDS MASS GRAVE OF SHIPWRECKED SLAVES and *The Express*: HELL OF SLAVE SHIP BOUND FOR DAMNATION. From the flames of these grisly titles the controversy spread like wildfire.

It was the beginning of a long and often bitter war of words in which I constantly found myself having to fight my way out of tight corners, desperately trying to argue that there was no evidence (which, ironically at that time there was not) that these people had been slaves. I asserted that they were just as likely to have been prisoners-of-war captured by the British during the French wars of the late 18th century. Inadvertently, I seemed to be feeding the media's frenzy. And yet it was the records, themselves, which had served to create the powerful images the stories now reflected. There were times when I began to feel that people held me to blame for accounts such as that recorded by Mrs Slade-King in 1879 (see page 12). Or the caption, for example below the painting which hangs in Ilfracombe Museum. This caption is evocative in itself and I quote it below for the benefit of the reader:

The old slaver 'London' from St Lucia in W. Indies, whilst attempting to enter Ilfracombe harbour was driven ashore in Rapparee & wrecked. She had been attached to Admiral Rodney's fleet in the W. Indies and was bringing home valuables & 150 slaves. 46 people were drowned 6 of whom were Ilfracombe seamen who went to their rescue.

This caption may be referring to the former use of the ship as a slaver and possibly had confused the term prisoners-of-war with slaves. Or so I thought at the time. In any event the seed was sown. The story was about to escalate.

§

While Roz and I were out there had been a telephone message from the Civic Centre in Barnstaple. Upon returning the call I was shocked to receive my first taste of hostility. I was not ready for the tone of the conversation during which it was demanded of me where I had received permission to dig the site. I stressed that such permission had been granted by North Devon District Council, knowing that it had been obtained via Jeanne at Ilfracombe Museum. This permission had been given verbally and when pressed the person concerned had assured us that his verbal permission was enough. I had never thought for a moment that this was likely to lead to any problems – after all Linda Blanchard, from North Devon District Council, had visited the site with me in her official capacity, prior to the excavation. While on site she had offered me a drawing frame to assist with the excavation, and true to her word, it was delivered to me by Nick Constable on the Saturday of the excavation.

So, why was it suddenly now being suggested that I did not have permission to dig? In addition Mrs Akers, whom Alison Mills had suggested I invite also arrived — and at the time she was Chairman, of *The North Devon Archaeological Society*. Gradually it became clear to me that the animosity I had felt was real as the controversy developed. Sides were clearly being taken.

At the time it seemed to me that the position was relatively clear. The various records were fairly accurate and differed only by degrees. The main issue as far as the media were concerned was whether the black people who had perished in the wreck were slaves or prisoners-of-war. I was happy to leave that issue to one side. I felt I had successfully proven that the wreck was *The London*, the date it had foundered, and approximately how many people were aboard. I was even confident that I knew that the ship was bound for Bristol . It materialised that some of the staff of North Devon Council had begun to argue that there was doubt concerning virtually all of the records. This left me convinced there was now a hidden agenda to discredit me. It is true that the frenzied activities of the preceding weeks had left me tired and one is always concerned about the possibility of paranoia — was this my imagination playing tricks? I am not naturally the sort of person to develop a complex overnight.

It was reported to me by the then Mayor of Ilfracombe that a woman had been interviewed on Radio Devon about the excavation. She had criticised virtually every aspect of the dig which I had undertaken. When the Mayor asked me what on earth was going on, I had to confess that I did not know. Apparently even my handling of the bones had been called into question, and yet up until that day all concerned had been complimenting me on my thoroughness and care, as well as the respect which everyone concerned had shown for what was — most importantly — a burial ground. I have been unable to obtain a copy of this interview on Radio Devon but the contents have been confirmed to me by several listeners. As it turned out the result was that I became ever more determined to find supporting evidence to uphold the validity of the records.

It was this determination that brought me to the notice of various people from the *African Reparations Movement* including Linda Bellos, who contacted me on Monday 24th February, telling me she had heard an interview during which she felt I had stood my corner well, despite being put under pressure.

Linda had began our discussion by saying how hostile, the radio presenter had seemed — several times abruptly cutting me off during the live interview. I agreed with Linda and explained that given a chance by the presenter, I had wanted to go on and say that the people who had drowned in the wreck deserved a respectful burial; that their bodies had been cast into the grave at the back of the cove in a manner which seemed to me to be sacrilegious.

The lack of respect for the people who had died at Rapparee worsened as time went on. During one interview a woman lost total interest in the story (prematurely, as subsequent documents have shown) when she became convinced that the victims were recorded as prisoners-of-war and not slaves. Interestingly this same woman claimed to be in receipt of a document which she was convinced confirmed that the drowned black people were *not* slaves. I was well aware of this document — bizarrely it was I who had agreed to her photocopying it from my file. Events were becoming a little crazy. Where the confusion was occurring was that some people seemed to think that I had stumbled across the bones in Rapparee Cove quite by chance and was blissfully unaware of any history surrounding their burial. The more I tried – as calmly as I could – to explain, they would interrupt me and begin lecturing me on subjects such as English Social History, Archaeology, Genealogy. Everyone, it seemed, knew far more than I did. They had all become experts on the wreck of *The London* in less than two weeks! I was shocked. I received long, rambling letters on the subject, almost all of which concluded by assuring me that the people who had drowned were absolutely *not*, and *never were* slaves.

Unwittingly, I had touched a nerve.

A call was put out for the city of Bristol to apologise for its past links with the slave trade, following which I was telephoned by someone from a radio station in Bristol, and informed that I had no evidence to support slavery ever having taken place in that city. I was dumbfounded and for once almost lost my temper: "One thing is for sure," I growled, through gritted teeth, "the people buried at Rapparee never took their place at Bristol!" My inference being that this was, after all, where the ship was bound.

Another radio presenter rang me and accused me of not having any evidence whatsoever — that the whole thing was '....a pack of lies!' From then on I was on my guard.

I was sent a copy of the Bristol *Evening Post* dated 27th February 1997, which featured a double page spread telling how :

the new Empire and Commonwealth Museum in Bristol is creating a fascinating archive which will tell us more about the trade in human flesh.

This 'fascinating archive' which filled two removal lorries, of course related to the slavery trade. The article discussed the anti-slavery campaigner William Wilberforce, and carried a picture of the the gravestone of Scipio Africanus, a former slave, and — amazingly — a photograph of the water colour by Walters 'The Wreck of *The London*' which hangs in Ilfracombe Museum. The controversy was further fuelled by a report which stated:

...Tests have since confirmed that the skulls are of Afro-Caribbean origin.

This was from *The Daily Telegraph*, 24th February and at that time was absolutely not the case. This all weighed heavily on my shoulders and I resolved to carry out further research. It was this research which led me to new evidence found in various archives in London.

§

Another story which appeared in the papers was entitled STORMS REVEAL GRIM LEGACY OF SLAVE TRADE. I read this headline and was thinking to myself *Oh No... It's going to be one of those days* when the telephone rang. It was Alison Mills and her tone was very friendly. I should make it clear, here, that the remains unearthed at Rapparee were at that moment stored at my home. The reason for this was simply that no official body had made a decision as to their ultimate fate. It had only been five days since the dig and my intention was that they should be moved as soon as possible to Ilfracombe Museum prior to proper expert analysis. Since then both myself and Roz, had come to believe that the council would rather have the bones on display in the North Devon Museum in Barnstaple. This would give the council control, and the chances were that the story would peter out or even be deliberately suppressed. It is possible that local government officials felt the ensuing international publicity had left them looking inert or even apathetic. I began to feel it was the council who were paranoid rather than me.

This reaction appeared to become more acute when the story attracted the attention of the MP Bernie Grant who had recently been involved in an exchange with the museum in Exeter concerning African bronze heads on display which had been obtained during Britain's

Colonial past. I guess somebody at North Devon District Council was keen to avoid a similar scenario. At the time I heard various comments to the effect that we should keep him away from North Devon if at all possible. It was just this sort of aside which spurred me on to confront the council at every opportunity.

Later that day, Joy Slocombe, from Ilfracombe Museum, passed a letter into my outer porch, which stated that a representative of North Devon Council intended to collect the remains the following morning, and that I should make arrangements to have them delivered to Ilfracombe museum in readiness.

I was incensed and immediately rang the the Museum of North Devon in Barnstaple to ask what they were playing at. I confess, that there ensued an unseemly shouting match during which it was demanded whether or not I was aware that North Devon District Council owned the bones. Blinded with anger I retorted : "So they are the *new* Slavemasters are they?"

Flatly, the answer came back, "We own the site."

I replied that the cove was part of Ilfracombe's history and, "The bones will stay in Ilfracombe."

It was then stated that, in fact, they wanted the bones displayed at Ilfracombe museum — in a place of public access. This had been my suggestion all along! The truth was, I suspected, that such public access would eventually mean the transferral of the bones to Barnstaple. The strain of recent times suddenly caught up with me and I exploded with rage, "You are not having the bones! They are staying here with me." With this I slammed the phone down. In effect the bones ultimately have ended up at Bristol University for DNA testing; however one full year on (as this book goes to press) there has still been no announcement concerning the results of any tests.

By now I had really had enough. The thought actually crossed my mind of loading all the remains into protective containers and driving off with them – where to, I do not know; but far away. It is very difficult for me to put into words my emotions at this time – I felt a great responsibility, aligned to an affinity with the remains which bordered upon the obligation one feels for their own family. I was genuinely concerned that the District Council should not assume control. The truth is, I do not know why I felt this way – it was an overpowering, intrinsic sense of duty. I am aware that by writing this I am giving the opposition a golden opportunity to scoff but I am in deadly earnest. I had been ridiculed by some sections of the media and dismissed by self-styled *experts*. I felt frustrated, exhausted and deeply worried. I was determined that North Devon District Council should not get hold of the remains under any circumstances. It was not possible that any person or institution could own them. How could they think in those terms?

Luckily, after a couple of hours I had cooled down and decided to seek some sound advice from two of my closest friends. I called them one after the other and they both offered the same wise counsel. Two of Ilfracombe's town councillors were telephoned on my behalf and they rallied to the cause. This helped pave the way when I personally contacted Ilfracombe's Mayor (incidentally, it was then that he told me of the woman who had criticised me on the radio interview).

The advice I received was that I should personally deliver the remains to Ilfracombe museum the next morning before it opened. Not to have done so would have left me open to legal action. I then phoned Jeanne Hardwick at the museum to arrange for delivery at 10am the next morning.

Very early on the day of delivery, I was telephoned by North Devon District Council's solicitor, who asked my intentions regarding the remains. He was extremely polite and after I had explained my proposal, he asked my opinion on the advisability of digging the site further. I told him that the bank above the site was at a 60 degree angle, and was unsafe to work under.

The day that Bernie Grant arrived (2nd March 1997) I was to find out that my suspicions regarding the proposed fate of the bones were true. I was now convinced that the intention was to move them to Barnstaple under the control of North Devon District Council. A member of the black press from Bristol telephoned me to ask what had been meant by a conversation he had overheard between two men and a woman outside Ilfracombe Museum:

We'll never get the bones back now Bernie Grant is involved — it will become a political issue.

During that week I received a phone call from Radio France, in Paris – I presume they were interested in the Napoleonic War element in the story but as – I am ashamed to say – I cannot speak a word of French the call ended on a farcical note. Next came my first phone call from a most pleasant lady named Rosetta Eligon at the Sancore Library in Bristol. She represents *Keyboard* – Bristol Churches working together for racial justice – and is both highly intelligent and deeply concerned about the implications surrounding the discovery of the bones.

Throughout that week the idea that the people who had drowned in the wreck of *The London* were predominantly prisoners-of-war and *not* slaves began to gain momentum. I was constantly pressured to assert this point of view as well as the view that we could not even be sure that they were from *The London*. It was suggested to me that it was imperative I make this statement. Yet, my assertion was that we could not (at that stage) be sure whether they were prisoners-of-war or slaves but that they *were*, beyond any reasonable doubt, from the wreck of *The London*.

The *Evening Post* in Bristol ran a story: THE TRAGIC CARGO in which they reported that I believed the drowned victims to have been listed as prisoners-of-war. There then followed a contradiction in the last paragraph when it stated:

> Mr Barrow believes the captain could have been worried about docking, in case the locals discovered the slaves on-board.

The same day the *Western Morning News* reported:
> Souvenir hunters risk lives at mass grave site.

North Devon District Council began warning of a risk to life, due to Monday's high seas disturbing the rocks. Apparently up to eight souvenir hunters were at the beach the previous day, and to prevent this the beach had been sealed off. This was done at the request of Bernie Grant MP, via a letter to the Department of National Heritage and Lord Inglewood, on 25th February

1997. In my opinion this was the right thing to do, and for the first time I felt that somebody else was sharing the responsibility. More people who genuinely cared for the people who had drowned were becoming involved. The relief was tremendous.

§

On the 27th February the front page headlines of the *North Devon Advertiser* read: MASS GRAVE ON HOLIDAY BEACH. The site was described as:
> The makeshift grave of dozens of hapless Napoleonic slaves.'

This was a very well researched and nicely written story. For once this reporter, Geoff Staddon, seemed to be interested in the truth and although it did nothing to resolve the slave *v* prisoner controversy it nonetheless summed up the known facts extremely well. In fact I rang the newspaper to express my thanks and from then on have been very friendly with the reporter. He has been kind enough to furnish me with some copies of photographs he took in my study at home where I had previously kept the bones. His report at the time also mentioned that the *African Reparation Movement* had approached North Devon District Council suggesting a formal re-burial.

The same day the *North Devon Journal* headline ran:
> RELICS OF SLAVE SHIP REVEALED BY SEA

Their report kindly mentioned that:
> ...local amateur Archaeologist Pat Barrow wants any artefacts preserved and hopes a memorial can be erected at the spot to mark the historic tragedy.

The inside feature in the same journal was headed:
> STORMS REVEAL SECRET OF SHIPWRECK.

The picture, with this story by Tahira Yaqoob, showed George Hardwick sieving out washed bone fragments. An echo of the animosity that I had encountered was reported where it stated:
> Pat Barrow, of Ilfracombe led an Archaeology hunt and discovered about 70 fragments of bone, teeth and iron

shackles. But Allen Loates, a spokesman for North Devon District Council, said: "Such digging could be seen as distasteful. Historical interest does not override the feeling that this is a sacred place to some people.

The site *is* a sacred place – to a lot of people, including myself. So the question has to be asked: Why is it that nothing had ever been done to protect, restore or investigate the site up until 22nd February 1997? Was it because North Devon District Council considered it *such* a sacred place? The fact that these people were buried at Rapparee Cove had been known to the powers-that-be for two-hundred years. It was reported in Parish magazines and local history books. PH Gosse had commented upon it. Mrs Slade-King and others had discussed it. The truth is, that in parts of sleepy, slippery North Devon many powerful people would far preferred to have *'let sleeping dogs lie'*.

The *North Devon Journal* article also mentioned my agreement with the suggestion that a memorial plaque should be set up overlooking Rapparee Cove and quoted a spokeswoman from Bernie Grant's office as saying that they were extremely interested in the discovery as the black community were becoming increasingly conscious of the whole history of slavery and the British involvement in it.

In response to a request from the same office for more information regarding the records I invited some of Mr Grant's colleagues to call at my house if they intended to visit Ilfracombe (as they had suggested) on Sunday 2nd March. I was promised a copy of a letter they had received from St Lucia about that island's local history, which duly arrived (see page 83).

All the people associated with Mr Grant's office as well as the *African Reparations Movement* gave me a great deal of support and were in genuine sympathy with my efforts to uncover the truth.

At about this time I gave a talk at Ilfracombe Junior School, and learnt how interested over a hundred children had been in the story – one of them was present at the cove when Peter Russell found the skull. The headmaster was also a keen wreck diver, and showed me some artefacts that had been salvaged from a Dutch wreck. In addition he showed me a Roman stone anchor.

Nigel Rigby from the *National Maritime Museum* called at Ilfracombe Museum. We discussed all the records that were available, then went over to the cove before returning to my house, where the ironwork was kept. Before he left he promised to send me some information about *The London* which he thought may be hidden in the archives at his place of work, and indeed this arrived, as promised (see pages 39 and 59).

This was indeed another busy day, and Stephen Cape from the BBC, rang me about the impending visit by Bernie Grant on 2nd March. This was actually the first confirmation I had that a visit was actually to take place.

That same day the Home Office sealed off the cove, and declared the site a war grave. However most locals ignored the barriers and continued to walk there, claiming that it was an ancient right of way. Still, a large percentage of people did obey the order, knowing it was not enforceable but avoiding the site out of respect.

Sharon Lawrence, who is Bernie Grant's secretary, telephoned to arranged with me to meet their group at Ilfracombe Museum on Sunday 2nd March, at 1pm.

I also received a letter from Philippa Gregory PhD from Midhurst, enclosing a copy of her book *A Respectable Trade* which concerns the slave trade in Bristol and was recently made into a widely acclaimed serial for the BBC. In addition I received a most heart-warming letter from Mrs Bunty Beresford of Bexhill-on-Sea. The sympathetic tone of this letter was such that, at the time, it was particularly welcome.

On 1st March, Jim Thompson from the BBC rang me about using my camcorder footage of the excavation; followed by another call from the BBC during which I was asked the nature of my connection with the *African Reparation Movement*. Of course, I had no connection with that organisation and I'm afraid my reply was rather short – "Respect for the dead".

I also had confirmation that day from Rosetta Eligon, from Bristol that she would also be coming over to Ilfracombe on 2nd March to meet Bernie Grant and she was bringing Mr Nabtali of the *Black Pyramid Film Company* with her.

7

The First Visit

The day had started with our friends, Richard and Marian Ashford arriving at my house, having walked over from Mortehoe along the Coastal Path. They had a cup of tea, freshened up and then changed into their best clothes before we left home at 12.30pm. I then drove down to Ilfracombe Museum with Roz in the front, and Richard and Marian Ashford sitting in the back with my stepdaughter Christine, who took photographs and video footage. A police car was already there, and so was Alison Mills with Mr Loates and Mr Morgan from North Devon District Council who both shook hands with me.

Roz and I were met by Doug Ray the Mayor, as planned, near the museum. From here we walked up to the main road and waited on the corner by the new Pavilion site, where we met Bernie Grant and his group at approximately 1.00pm. I shook the MP's hand, and said "Hello, I'm Pat Barrow, Mr Grant..."

He smiled, and asked "How are you?" and I replied "Very well thank you."

Doug Ray then shook his hand and announced, "I'm the Mayor."

Embarrassed by my lack of formality I stammered, "Oh I'm sorry I forgot to introduce him to you."

After some good natured laughter my group climbed back into the Nissan and we led the way to the pier car park, with Mr Grant and his colleagues following in their vehicle. We passed the boats dotted about waiting for repairs before finally stopping against the far fence which had just been erected to seal off the pier, because it had become dangerous. We clambered out to greet two local New Labour party officials, Annie Brenton (North Devon) and David Brenton (Torridge and West Devon). The press were now in hot pursuit.

I then presented Mr Grant with a green plastic folder containing photographs of the cove taken at various angles and distances. At this time the site could not be visited because the cove was closed to the public. He took the folder and thanked me, before announcing to the press that he very much wanted to hear local opinion regarding the bones. He then turned to me and asked me what I thought should happen to them, and I answered:

"Well... we have thought about this and I think it would be a lovely idea to send the bones back to St. Lucia and their descendants — but what about the remains that may still be buried in the slope, it would be a great shame to separate them."

The MP then said that he agreed with my comment. Next he told the press about the importance of the local peoples' point of view; and how the wreck in the cove was also part of their history. We then climbed half-way up Lantern Hill in order to view the cove across the water. Mr Grant looked across the bay with his binoculars and one of his colleagues followed suit, taking up the offer to borrow our binoculars. The MP was studying the cove with intense serenity, and his emotion was clear to see.

Various group photos were taken, and several interviews given, before we proceeded back down the winding path of Lantern Hill. On the way down I chatted with Sharon, Mr Grant's secretary, and other members of his group. I was introduced to Linda Bellos later, back at the museum, where we had gathered for a press conference

As we approached the museum in our various vehicles, I put my hand out to signal where we intended to park and the policewoman on duty smiled warmly, and I smiled back. This indicated to me how well the day was going and as we all entered the museum we were greeted enthusiastically by Joy Slocombe the curator.

I was glad to meet Rosetta Eligon of *Bristol Churches Working Together For Racial Justice* and Mr Nabtali of the *Black Pyramid Film Company* who had just arrived at the museum. Mr Grant was noticeably moved as he viewed the bones and he thanked Joy for her consideration and hospitality and donated £50 to the museum. As various members of his group mingled with the crowd and chatted, Mr Grant signed the visitors book, and commented:

"What a beautiful place Ilfracombe is."

The press were told how the *African Reparation Movement* would like a ceremony to be held each year on Emancipation Day — 1st August. I thought what a wonderful opportunity this would be for Ilfracombe, relying as it does upon visitors to boost the local economy. In addition there was the date of the wreck itself — October 9th. Clearly this was the beginning of something great for all concerned.

Later, we all went back to our house in a convoy of cars. Roz prepared tea and scones with Devonshire Clotted Cream and jam, which was heartily enjoyed by all. Joy appeared to be missing so we rang the museum and asked her to come over, which she did.

Bernie Grant wrote a note to Roz and myself, which reads as follows:

To: Pat & Rosamund. It has been a pleasure being here. Thanks for the hospitality and the digging. All the best , your friend, Bernie Grant MP. 2-3-97.

I believe it is safe to say that the whole day was a resounding success. I received an official letter of thanks, dated 3rd March 1997 on House of Commons note paper , and was worded as follows:

I am writing to thank you very much for all your kindness on Sunday. Clearly without your hard work and inquisitiveness, we should never have known about the discovery at Rapparee Cove, or indeed the wreck of 'The London' itself. We are extremely grateful to you. May I also say how kind it was of you to invite us back to your house, and on behalf of ARM, thank you for giving us such a warm welcome and such a delicious tea. We look forward to seeing you again before too long, and trust you will keep in touch in the meantime.

Yours sincerely,

Bernie Grant,
MP for Tottenham.

The day following the visit, on the 3rd March, a gentleman from the Home Office rang Jeanne Hardwick
at Ilfracombe Museum, and complained to her that
permission had not been given to dig the site. Jeanne
explained that we had verbal permission, from North
Devon District Council and that she had been assured
that written permission was not needed. It was then
stated to Jeanne that digging a war-grave, or removing
human bones, was not allowed without special permission.

Yet the coroner and the police were fully aware of the
find, and had not expressed any concern, other than
what is normal in such cases, with regard to the excavation of 22nd February. We had been careful to follow the
rules as they had been explained to us. The site was not
declared a war-grave until after controversy had been
fuelled by the press and this was after the partially
excavated. The man from the Home-Office went on to
state that he believed we had acted in ignorance and
there was likely to be no further action. It must be
repeated again, that the authorities knew of the bones
often unearthed at Rapparee Cove even if they were
unaware from where they came. The wall at the back of
the cove had been down since at least 1991 so why was
it not rebuilt earlier? Clearly the only concern of the
authorities is 'bad' publicity.

And such publicity continued on apace. A friend of
mine, Chuck Warwick, told me he had heard the bones
referred to on Radio Devon as 'Barrow's Bones'.

On the 4th March, Lucy McKeith contacted me. She
had previously arranged a meeting in Exeter regarding
holocaust victims, and was thinking of doing something
similar for the victims at Rapparee whom she believed
were either slaves or Freemen from St Lucia who were
being returned to England to become slaves again. She
spoke of raising funds for another, more detailed excavation to recover any remaining bones. She talked of her
ideas for a celebration of freedom which could include an
African band, in honour of the victims' ancestry. She
was extremely motivated and willing to help in any way.
The emotion she relayed when discussing the subject
was extremely touching.

Joy rang me at 3pm on 5th March to say that Alison Mills had arrived at the museum with a young lady who was a bone specialist, could I please come down at once.

When I arrived I found the museum full of students of many nationalities, all milling around studying the various exhibits. The atmosphere was warm and genial as Joy greeted me with her usual bright smile. I was led into her small room where I was introduced by Alison to Dr Juliet Cross, the skeletal specialist. We began to discuss the whole issue, and how politics were now revolving around the subject, and how best to study the bones in a scientific way.

I asked Juliet what she thought should happen and she explained that she would like to conduct research on the bones, if everyone agreed. She then had a brief look at the bones and said that in her opinion some of the bones were from a young person under the age of 15 years. She later did more detailed research and produced a report entitled: *The human skeletal material from Rapparee Cove. A report on the material recovered in February 1997. Dr J F Cross April 1997.* This report can be seen in Ilfracombe Museum, with the permission of the curator.

No further discussion took place that day regarding the ultimate fate of the bones as I had to be at Ilfracombe Comprehensive School by 4pm, where I was meeting Anne Davies to arrange a talk I was giving in the Lantern Centre about the history of Rapparee Cove.

§

The 6th March started with an article in the *North Devon Advertiser*, headed :

BEACH BONES CONTROVERSY

Mystery is building up over Ilfracombe bones on the beach as the question is asked: Were they really those of victims of the slave trade?

This was the beginning of a new round of publicity which I believe was being engineered to debunk the theory that those who had perished in the wreck of *The London* were, or ever had been slaves. It began to dawn on me that as fast as I produced evidence to back my claims; such evidence was being deemed inadmissable. At this stage, and on balance, I believed myself that the victims were probably prisoners-of-war and not slaves yet I was confused as to why doubt was being cast upon the evidence as to the name of the ship and date of the wreck. It seemed that the whole story had to be disproved — at all and any cost. What could never be denied was the validity of the records. For 200 years these bodies had lain hidden, buried in the cove — they were not only heroes from the St Lucian Islands, but were now part and parcel of the history of Ilfracombe. Whatever the truth it should be jointly acknowledged, and not denied. Ilfracombe was now the link between the original homeland of these people – Africa – and the land which had been forced upon them or their parents – St Lucia. To claim that all the evidence is suspect is nothing more than a clever attempt to mitigate the horror of it all. Whether or not the victims were technically classed as slaves when the ship wrecked; or whether they had been temporarily granted their freedom by the French so they could help prosecute the war against the English in the Carribean is at best a mute point. I cannot believe that people who drowned —men, women and children — chained below decks as *The London* was dashed against the rocks, can be denied a shrine because two hundred years later bureaucrats are not convinced that technically these people were slaves. I then began to wonder whether, if *The London* had not wrecked, but had continued on to Bristol, whether any new-found freedom of the black prisoners in the hold would have been honoured. How would they be classified when they arrived at Stapleton Prison in Bristol? In this way I stumbled upon a fact that was to make me even less popular with the 'powers-that-be.'

The idea of a shrine as a permanent memorial to the people who drowned at Rapparee Cove was on one hand gaining momentum. On the other hand it was being played down.

§

Later that same day, Joy rang me to say that the High Commissioner of St Lucia, Aubrey Hart was arriving in Ilfracombe on the following Wednesday. The St Lucians had obviously become concerned at reports they had received regarding the bones and the fact that they may belong to their ancestors. Joy asked if I would be prepared to help welcome him to the Museum, which of course I was delighted to do.

Many people were now showing an emotional interest and the following day when I called in at the Museum I met Maxine Jarrett, who had travelled down from London especially to see the bones, and find out more about the story. She had been so moved by one newspaper report that she sent out twenty copies to her friends. Maxine told me she had trained as a journalist with Dave McCalla, of the *Voice* newspaper in Bristol, and was presently an Architectural Photographer. I was taken aback by the depth of her emotion and left the museum in a sombre mood though strangely elated that I had met her.

The same day the *North Devon Journal* was reporting:

JUSTICE CALL FOR SHIPWRECK SLAVES. :

MP Bernie Grant visited North Devon at the weekend and said African slaves who drowned there should be commemorated with a memorial.

He suggested a memorial be placed in Ilfracombe together with an annual service held on Emancipation Day.

Official confirmation of the bones' origin has still not been made but they are thought to be those of slaves.

Mr Grant said : "This is an important find for black British history because it demonstrates that Britain was very much involved in the slave trade."

"Before I came down and spoke to the local people I felt that if possible, the remains of those people should be sent back to the country they came from. However, local people feel that there should be a memorial set up here and I think we would support that."

"The Labour Party believes in justice for all and that includes people who have not had justice for some considerable time" he said.

On 7th March there was an interesting comparison made in the *Western Morning News* by Graham Danton, entitled:

EXPRESSING OUR SHAME ON SLAVERY

Mr Grant wants the Queen to apologise for slavery, and he has a point. If we expect the Japanese to apologise for their brutal enslavement of our POWs, we must also express shame at exploiting man's greatest insult, indignity and cruelty to his fellow beings, for over two centuries.

That evening I was interviewed by Radio Leicester and, as usual the question of slavery topped the list. I answered as honestly as I could.

On 8th March Simon Hewitt from Birmingham, rang me, and I arranged to meet him and his friend Janine, that weekend. We met at Ilfracombe Museum and had a thoroughly interesting talk, since Simon lectures in African history. We had some photos taken together next to the painting by Walters, and had lunch with Janine and Roz in a local fish restaurant *The Red Petticoat* which we thoroughly enjoyed. Simon put details of the story on the Internet for all to contact, and we have corresponded several times since.

Later that day I had arranged to meet Alison Mills, to visit the cove as she wanted me to point out where various items had been found. I was disappointed later, when she released a report about the site entitled:
Bones found at Rapparee Cove, Summary of Historical and Archaeological Evidence.

In the copy given to me Alison had handwritten on an introductory slip that her report was 'cynical'. In the report, itself, she states:
I understand that DNA analysis requires samples to be excavated with great care, and the Rapparee bones will have been contaminated.

It had never occurred to me that the report would be critical of my involvement in the 22nd February excavation. In fact during later, professional archaeological excavations, I noted that the bones uncovered were handled in exactly the same way and I could not have handled the bones with any more care or respect.

It appeared, now, that even the attribution of race was going to be difficult, and yet DNA taken from pulp deep inside teeth, where contamination from external sources would be hard pressed to reach, *is actually* possible. This was later confirmed by Dr Mark Horton of Bristol University Archaeological Dept.

Later in her report it is interesting to note that Alison had written that the coins from the cove:

were mostly Portuguese and Spanish and ranged in date from the late 17th century to 1784. If all these were from the same wreck, it must be later than 1784-possibly The London, or perhaps other vessels such as The Phoenix, wrecked in 1810 on a voyage from Oporto to Bristol.

Yet some of the coins found had been used for an exhibition organised by Alison in St. Ann's Chapel, in Barnstaple in 1991, and at that time all the evidence I had gathered over the years was used to construct the captions put on various exhibits. Such captions widely supported the idea that the coins came from the wreck of *The London*. I was concerned now, that doubt was being cast on the origins of the coins. I still have one of the captions that was used in the 1991 exhibition, and it reads as follows:

We can choose how much of this account to believe, but it does tell us one thing. The wreck of 'The London' in 1796 is almost certainly the source of some, if not all the coins found at Rapparee Cove. It also caused the deaths of many men who fought for their freedom in the West Indies, and may have preferred death to the new slavery that awaited them.'

It is important that in all the shipwrecks reported at or near Ilfracombe over the centuries none have ever been associated with finds of gold coins, jewellery or treasure of any kind other than the reports regarding *The London*. There is no reason to doubt that *The London* was the ship involved, as there is no doubt that it was carrying black prisoners and it was carrying a large amount of treasure.

Alison partly concluded her report with the words:

*The story of The London is an interesting one and,
with the help of historians in the West Indies and
Bristol, it may be possible to put together an account
of the final journey.*

No mention is made that any local historian may help in
solving the riddle. Lots of people in Ilfracombe had given
lots of their time freely, and with good heart, in a
genuine attempt to uncover the truth surrounding the
wreck of *The London*. I was surprised and saddened that
we were precluded.

§

A report dated 13th March now appeared in the *North
Devon Journal*, headed:

BONES MAY NOT BE FROM SLAVE SHIP :

*North Devon District Council spokesman Allan Loates
said the bones may be from prisoners-of-war brought
back by the British fleet in the wars which raged from
1800 to 1815.*

This statement would clearly rule out *The London* as
being the ship from which the bodies came — if it were
correct. The wreck of *The London* was in 1796 and this
statement gives the dates 1800-1815. According to
Steinberg's *Dictionary of British History* the French
Revolutionary and Napoleonic Wars 'raged' between the
years 1793-1815, and Britain's involvement in them
stemmed from a dispute affecting maritime and commer-
cial interests. What became known as 'the war of the
first coalition' was characterised by a lavish dispersal of
British effort when Prime Minister Pitt mainly used
British naval predominance to overrun the French West
Indian sugar islands and ruin French trade. Guadeloupe
and St Lucia were captured in 1794 and command of the
sea was emphasised by the establishment of a base on
Haiti. However, refusal by the Afro-Carribean population
of these islands to concede produced serious difficulties
and between 1794-1796 British casualties were 80,000
— more even than the Peninsular campaign.
    In an extract from a document kindly sent from the
St Lucian Islands by Mr Len Waite a closer examination

can be made concerning events on the island of St Lucia during 1796. This document is from a magazine (National Trust) which deals with the history of St Lucia and is currently being used to show that traditional Colonial history may have been less than balanced in its interpretation of events. The object is to provide an objective view for the children of that area to study :

Last month, we looked at events in St Lucia in the year 1796, 200 years ago when the British Army under General Abercromby, arrived to take back the island from a force of ex-slaves. These men had rebelled against the harsh treatment meted out under colonial rule by both the British and the French in turn, as each country took possession of St Lucia.

The year before, 1795, the rebels had defeated the British in a series of battles at Pigeon Island, the Vigie and Fort Charlotte, which used to be on the top of Morne Fortune, overlooking Castries Bay. In the days of sail St Lucia was not only strategically placed for foreign fleets to control the Caribbean Sea and the underside of the (later) USA, but it possessed, in Castries, the finest deep water port in the Caribbean.

Abercromby landed his three armies [in 1796] at Longuiville Bay; Choc Bay and the last at Anse la Raye....

Of course the above does not prove that the bodies found at Rapparee Cove are from the wreck of *The London*. I fully believe that evidence I have since uncovered and refer to later in this book will, however, do so. I quote the above only to show how odd it is to try and push the possible dates for the bodies *on from* 1796. On what possible evidence does *that assumption* lie?

On the same day as the *North Devon Journal* report I was in the museum when Philippa Gregory PhD, arrived with her husband. I showed them the water-colour of *The London* by J Walters. I had previously been looking at a copy of another – almost identical – painting by G Walters (1811-1882). It occurred to me that two artists had been inspired to paint their interpretation of the dramatic wrecking of *The London* and yet modern public officials seemed equally determined to belittle the drama.

In the G Walters version the ship was more on the rocks and the rowing boat was further out; one of the people observing the spectacle is pointing in the ship's direction. Later, after Philippa had copied some details from *The London* file we all left, and visited the cove. Rosamund was already there talking to four Birmingham people about the bones.

We continued on down to the site, leaving Roz up at the top by the benches with two of the women she had been talking to. We discussed the ballast (Gosse, 1853) that is said to have been from the wreck, and I told Philippa about the child's bones. She suggested to me that the presence of remains of young people may be more likely to suggest a connection with slavery because younger – rather than older – people were used for this purpose. I then summarised my conclusions regarding the events which had led to the wreck and the burial of the people at Rapparee.

On 14th March I called at the museum to pick up some documents I had left there the day before, and an Australian journalist called Ross Cameron from Queensland, was talking to Jeanne about the controversy. He asked me to explain how and why I had reached the conclusions I had and I did so as best I could. I pointed out especially that the records were difficult to prove and how the media seemed at one time intent on exploiting the rather more sensational idea that the people who had drowned on *The London* were slaves; and how recently the tide had turned and more emphasis was being laid on the idea that the people were either prisoners-of-war or from a different ship altogether. He was convinced that I was right to continue to fully establish the truth of the story one way or the other and he advised me: "Stay in there and fight it." — Mr Cameron had been voted Investigator of the Year in 1987. I fully intended to follow his advice.

§

The HTV Documentary
April 1997

Dr Juliet Cross the skeletal biologist arrived again at the Ilfracombe Museum about on Good Friday, 28th March, whist I was talking to Joy and Jeanne at the front desk. Joy and Jeanne were happy to see her, having been telephoned earlier by Alison Mills to advise them of Dr Cross's visit. She was re-assessing the bones in preparation for a HTV documentary which was to be directed by Jane Ryder. Dr Cross reaffirmed to me that the fragments she had looked at were from three bodies. Some of the bones were from a child of junior school age, perhaps as young as 4-8 years old.

The following Tuesday Joy rang me to say that Jane Ryder had arrived, and could I come down right away. Pausing only to grab my files, I drove down to the museum where I was introduced to Jane and the commentator, Richard. We discussed in some detail the results of my research and then along with the camera man, sound engineer and the lighting man we headed along the sea front to the cove car-park. From here the recording equipment was carried down into the cove, and set up at the site where the bones had been found. I was filmed lightly scraping back the shingle whilst being interviewed by Richard. Shots were taken from various angles and from the top of the steps looking down into the cove.

They also took various shots of the sea entrance to the cove – views I knew would be spectacular on the screen because the sun was shining, and the sky bright blue. The air was warm providing you were standing out of the brisk wind, and when filming was finally finished we all headed back to the museum, where the crew had arranged to meet Juliet and Alison at 1pm.

Joy greeted us warmly, and arrangements were made for filming the bones, whilst Dr. Cross was interviewed about the results of her study.

Next Alison Mills was interviewed and stated that in her opinion the issue of wreck of *The London* was less important than establishing the definite origin of the bones as the people of St Lucia had expressed a desire to have them returned to that island:

'...*provided that is, they actually came from the island*.'

Alison appeared to be far from convinced that they did originate from St Lucia. In addition she was not convinced that the records from which I had constantly been quoting were accurate.

Where Alison and I differed was whether there was sufficient proof that these bones were the bones of prisoners (formerly slaves) and that they had perished during the wreck of *The London.*

We needed proof regarding an accurate date of the age of the bones and the main problem with acquiring this is that Radio Carbon can not be used in this case – the groundwater that had been percolating through the site for so many years has left modern organic matter deposited in the bones – from plants that had died recently for example, as the water flowed down from the field above. This has the effect of achieving a Radio Carbon date that is too recent. In addition materials less than two hundred years old are too modern for Radio Carbon dating, due to the relatively recent pumping of unusually high levels of carbon into the atmosphere.

During the interview I contended that at least if *this* test was carried out we could rule out a more ancient date for the bones. It began to appear to me that the money for such a test would only be forthcoming if the results were likely to prove my conclusions were *not* accurate. The point was made bluntly to me – and I do not make this assertion lightly – that the money would not be made available simply to prove that my conclusions were accurate. I felt at this point that the film crew looked distinctly uncomfortable.

The painting of the wreck of *The London* was filmed next, whilst Joy and Jeanne were again rushed off their feet dealing with the general public. Joy and Jeanne deserve a lot of credit for all the extra work and effort they have had to endure as a result of the publicity surrounding Rapparee Cove. A duty they perform at all times with great enthusiasm and cheerfulness.

I enjoyed a late lunch with Richard and Jane and the crew – again at the *Red Petticoat* – and I am happy to say it was a thoroughly enjoyable meal after which we all returned to the museum.

Joy had gone home for the day and Jeanne was in charge. Jeanne had done some research into John Chiswell's family history ready for HTV's documentary (see page 37) and I was to be filmed standing next to his gravestone at the Parish Church. At the graveside we discussed John Chiswell's role in the 1856 account as a witness for the correspondent of the *North Devon*

Journal, and in another scene I answered questions about John Chiswell's role as a pilot in connection with the wreck of *The London.*

HTV sent me a copy of the whole of the documentary filmed in Ilfracombe which now blended interviews with Bernie Grant MP and Mr Ben Bousquet, who is a councillor as well as a St Lucian historian and with a Bristol historian regarding Stapleton Prison. Bristol was *The London's* intended destination at the time of the wreck and ultimately where some of the survivors were taken. A letter written to Richard Allard who was the governor of this prison in 1796 is dated 27th October and reads as follows:

'We have given directions to hire a small vessel for carrying between 30 & 40 sick French prisoners from Ilfracombe, where they are now, to Bristol. As they are chiefly, if not all, naturals of the West Indies, we direct you to make what they suffer as little as possible from the coldness of the season.'

8

The Bristol Connection

On 25th February 1997 Bernie Grant MP had sent an official letter to Lord Inglewood, at the Department of National Heritage, Cockspur Street London. In this Mr Grant writes of his concern at reports of souvenir hunters 'at the recently uncovered graveyard of 60 slaves in Rapparee Cove, Ilfracombe in North Devon'.

In the same letter he writes:

...in view of this, and the sensitive nature of the findings, I would be obliged if you would consider assisting the North Devonshire County Council in securing the site.

I believe Mr Grant was suggesting fencing off the site only where the bones had been found and not the whole of Rapparee Cove, which is how the council interpreted his request.

The rest of Mr Grant's letter is worth recording here, and reads as follows:

In view of the high level of interest that this finding has attracted, in particular from black people in Britain, may I suggest that the site be declared a National Heritage Site, and a memorial erected in honour of the slaves that perished there in 1796. I would be grateful if you would consider this proposal and let me have your thoughts.

The reply came back from Lord Inglewood on 18th March 1997, addressed to Bernie Grant Esq. MP:

'Thank you for your letter date 25th February about the recently uncovered grave, believed to be of 60 slaves from St Lucia, at Ilfracombe in Devon. I have followed with great interest the press reports about this site and your recent visit.'

'Protection for buried human remains is provided under the Burials Act 1857, which requires that a license must be obtained before they can be removed. However, a license can be issued retrospectively when remains have had to be removed following natural disturbance. The Home Office have been in touch with North Devon District Council and Ilfracombe Museum to guide them on this. I understand that some of the remains are currently being analysed to identify their likely origin.'

'Regarding making the beach secure, the local authority cannot prevent people visiting the site but have nevertheless put up very clear danger signs as the beach is now unsafe, following cliff erosion and recent storms. Although some 'souvenir' hunters have been known about for sometime and that in the past only a few coins have been found, mainly at low tide.'

Since that time Mr Grant has written me another letter concerning new proposals in connection with erecting a monument in Rapparee Cove:

Re: Rapparee Cove Site.

Further to our telephone conversation of Friday 4th April, I thought I should put on paper some of the issues we discussed and what I consider could be a way forward in the future. Once again, I would like to thank you and the people of Ilfracombe for dealing with this matter so sensitively and I hope that the co-operation that has been demonstrated so far will continue in the future.

First of all we have been inundated with offers of assistance from many people including professionals who want to get involved in some way. These professionals are both black and white and rang from historians and archaeologists to ordinary people who would like to be involved. It seems to me that one way of involving these volunteers, and those people who have contacted you also, would be to have some sort of conference in Ilfracombe. We could invite them to come down and have local, regional and national experts address the conference and by general consensus of those attending, plus the local community, we can put forward plans for the development of the site. I would envisage that such a conference could take place in the late summer after the 1st of August commemoration that we are planning. I would be obliged if you could let me know if you think that this is a reasonable proposal. If so, please let me know whether Ilfracombe has the facility to host such a conference, which I expect to be of no more than forty people, how much it would cost for the accommodation of these people and what time you think would be most suitable for such a conference.

I would hope that a conference such as this would address the issues of research, both here and in St Lucia, if St Lucia turns out to be the country from which they came; the question of a memorial, probably on top of the cliff above Rapparee Cove; and also the question of annual pilgrimage to the site.

If you agree with the above, I would be obliged if you could also let me have a list of the people who you believe should be involved from Ilfracombe and other regional areas.'

Clearly Mr Grant has not only the interests of the descendants of the people who perished in mind, but also those of the local people too. He is indeed a considerate and caring man. His sincerity in the matter was demonstrated when he visited Ilfracombe, and how deeply moved he was on that occasion was plain to see. Since February I had kept Mr Grant informed both of the progress of my investigations into the old records surrounding the wreck of *The London* and the debate which was now being waged concerning whether those who had died were slaves or prisoners-of-war. I had considered the point that the people from St Lucia (or their close ancestors) had been slaves from Africa. The *African Reparation Movement* were keen to stress this point, and rightly so. I saw them now as my only allies outside of my circle of friends in Ilfracombe.

An equally sympathetic interest was now shown by the St Lucian government.

The High Commissioner of St Lucia Visits Ilfracombe.

On 12th March at 12.30pm, Joy rang me to say that the High Commissioner of St Lucia, Aubrey Hart, had arrived at the museum.

I was keen to show my complete file on *The London* to Ben Bousquet, who was a councillor as well as a St Lucian historian and had accompanied the commissioner in their chauffeured limousine. When we arrived at the museum, it was bustling with a party of school children and their teacher. Jeanne Hardwick greeted us in the thick of the crowd, and led us around to the room next to the office, where I shook hands with the commissioner and Mr Bousquet before introducing them to my wife Rosamund. We immediately began to discuss the records and Mr Bousquet explained that the West Indians from St Lucia were not slaves — that they had been freed in 1783, by the French; and had fought hard against the English who referred to them as *Brigands*.

I had been fortunate in obtaining some information concerning the ultimate fate of the *Brigands* captured by the English during the French Revolutionary Wars in the Caribbean, from John Penny of *Fishponds Local History Society* who in turn had obtained the information from two documents referring to the history of Stapleton Prison. These documents are *Registers of POWs at Bristol* in the Public Records Office at Kew and an article by Dorothy Vinter in the 1956 *Transactions of the Bristol & Gloucestershire Archaeological Society*. Part of the information supplied to me by Mr Penny read as follows:

....*the Stapleton prisoners remained unhappy, overcrowded and underfed. They were mainly French sailors, counted literally in thousands, recruited in the great ports of France, but also in the French West Indies so that many were coloured men. In the first three years of war numbers had increased from one thousand to nearly two thousand, while a further 90 officers and 700 French troops captured in Ireland arrived in 1796 to which were added some of the 4000 West Indian prisoners taken by Lord Abercromby...*

Mr Bousquet confirmed that he had been puzzling for 20

years about where the prisoners had been taken. His accounts from the island only record that the prisoners had been taken out to the ships in the bay, to be transported — and not their destination. Thankfully, I had also obtained a photocopy of an account in the 1796 *Sherbourne Mercury* (dated October 4th), which cites a letter from Lord Grenville to the Lord Mayor of London which discusses the fact that 3000 prisoners had left the island of St Lucia, on *The Ganges* convoy:

> *The homeward bound West India Fleet is safe arrived at Crookhaven, without the loss of a single ship under convoy of the Ganges, of 74 guns, consisting of 103 vessels. Some parted on their passage bound for Liverpool, &c. the remainder about 70 put into Crookhaven. They left the West Indies on the 27th July, and have brought home about 3000 prisoners, the most of which are blacks, with two Generals.*

I told Ben that the location of the port called Crookhaven had been difficult to trace, but a bay called Crook is near the Stapleton area of Bristol, and if ships put into that place then it would be natural for Lord Grenville to term it Crookhaven.

Ben was puzzled, because there had been five generals according to him, so he asked me, "where were the other three taken?" I then reminded him that according to the John Penny account 4000 West Indian prisoners had ultimately been taken to the Bristol prison, and suggested that the other three Generals may have been with the remaining 1000, perhaps in another convoy.

I wanted Mr Bousquet and the High Commissioner to see the cove as it was at high tide, so they could see how it was transformed into a walled inlet and I asked Joy to put on a video tape I had recorded that morning and we were joined by various local government officials. The video showed the 9.9m high tide at 8.13am, the tide just lapping the base of the site wall, but the sea was calm, so waves did not crash onto the site.

The Commissioner stated that his government was interested in the site, but he was keen that nobody should go off "half cocked as it were". Mr Bousquet then told the history of his own interest, and that of another historian called Robert DeVaux (of the *National Archives*, Vigie, Castries St Lucia) who was designing a monument to be erected in 'Heroes Park', to be unveiled in June 1998. Then a local councillor, Jill Withers, spoke on behalf of Ilfracombe council and told how they would be prepared to contribute towards the cost of a memorial to be erected in the cove. The Mayor of Ilfracombe Doug Ray then thanked them, and Barry Bradshaw later suggested twinning with the island of St Lucia.

Jill Withers then announced that we were all to go to dinner at *The London and Paris* restaurant, and the Mayor arranged for the police to organise a parking space for the Commissioner's limousine, and the car in which Roz and I travelled with a trustee of Ilfracombe Museum, Michael Bale. Aubrey Hart and Ben Bousquet signed the museum visitors' book as we left.

The meal was a great success with a main course of seared salmon with a ginger sauce and salad or chips. Afterwards we all drove over to the cove, to inspect the site where the bones had been found.

At the top of the cove we paused beside the grassed area before descending the steps. This was the location which I suggested would be ideal to erect a monument. The open area could resemble a garden with plenty of room for people to gather, and perfect for an annual ceremony. Then we viewed the position which is now occupied by the seats (known locally as *the high balcony*), which Michael Bale suggested as another possible location for the monument. This situation, also, would be extremely good.

Then our group proceeded down on to the shingle of the cove where I picked up a yellow pebble and gave it to the Commissioner, explaining that this was part of what is reputed to be the gravel ballast from *The London*, referred to by P H Gosse (see page 10). I asked him if he had ever seen this type of rock on the island of St Lucia, and he confirmed that it was very familiar and would investigate further when he was back on the island.

I then conducted the group to the eroded site and pointed out a small piece of lime which could be seen near the bottom of the bank. In his letter to me, John Penny had discussed the appaling burial procedures for prisoners at Stapleton during the French wars, and following an extension to the building (which is now Blackberry Hill Hospital) in the 1950s, Mr Penny had personally found several skulls and numerous bones –

the remains of prisoner burials – which had been thrown into rough unmarked graves within the prison walls:

...but the powers that be [in the 1950s] took little notice and did all they could to make sure as few people as possible found out about it!

Another part of the documents relating to Stapleton reveal the following:

....the bodies were placed in piles (with white lime and canvas only), head to foot, to save space and three groups of skeletons buried in this way have been found.

This reference to white lime was playing on my mind as I had often noticed the lime lying in undisturbed parts of the bank at Rapparee. There is no conclusive evidence that lime was used in the burials of the black prisoners from *The London* but it is interesting that a painting by J Jackson of Barnstaple dated 1835 clearly shows an operating limekiln within 200 yards of the site of the burials at Rapparee.

§

A letter was later sent to Joy at the museum, headed:

HIGH COMMISSION FOR EASTERN CARIBBEAN STATES

I write in reference to my visit to Ilfracombe and in particular to your wonderful museum, on Wednesday, March 12, 1997

Please accept my sincerest gratitude for the particularly warm welcome and many courtesies extended to Ben Bousquet and myself. It was really beyond expectation.

The arrangements and other forms of assistance from different levels of the towns administration could not have been better.

It would be greatly appreciated if you could convey these sentiments to your staff at the museum as well as Mr and Mrs Pat Barrow. I will be writing to the Lord Mayor to express my appreciation.

May I ask you to send me copies of the relevant reports of the sinking of The London, along with any documentation of related events including the discovery of the bone fragments. Pictures of the bone fragments, if available would be also helpful.

I look forward with much anticipation to another perhaps more leisurely visit to your most picturesque and friendly town.

Yours sincerely

Aubrey E Hart.
High Commissioner,

Later, Ben Bousquet contacted Dr Mark Horton of Bristol University, regarding the possibility of having the bones scientifically dated. It is important to establish once and for all that they *are* from the wreck of *The London* and more importantly from St Lucia. Mark Horton is a Doctor of Archaeology and we had been advised that he was interested in further excavating the site. In addition there has been tentative discussion regarding a proposed formal meeting with Alison Mills, the North Devon District Council, Joy Slocombe, Ben Bousquet, Bernie Grant and myself regarding the site and the bones. To date, though, this has not happened and we are no further forward in knowing their ultimate fate, and whether they are to be returned to St Lucia. This stalemate will probably continue until the funds are provided to finally establish the date that the bones were buried in the cove.

§

Then the following letter arrived confirming the St Lucian government's keen interest.

A letter dated 25th March 1997 was received by the Mayor of Ilfracombe, councillor D. Ray from Government House in St Lucia which reads as follows:

His Worship the Mayor.
Councillor D.Ray.
Council Offices.
Northfield Road.
Ilfracombe EX 34 8AL.
United kingdom.
Your Worship,
I have received the news within the last couple weeks that the remains of Shipwrecked slaves were recently uncovered on a holiday beach in North Devon. I am also advised that further excavations have unearthed the bones of more bodies than we originally thought to have been there.

Councillor Ben Bousquet has provided some of this information and I wish to express my gratitude and that of my government for your co-operation and any assistance that you can give in arranging for the proper disposal of the remains, in England or in St Lucia.

Even before this news, our National Trust had already identified a site to be dedicated to the Brigands who courageously fought as freedom fighters in battles between the British and French in St Lucia in the years between 1794 and 1797. A token of the remains discovered could be returned to St Lucia to be buried at this site which incidentally is to be located near an existing Monument to the Inniskilling Regiment who fought with General Moore against the Brigands and the French in 1796 to recapture Morne Fortune in St Lucia.

I thank you for such assistance as you can extend on this amazing discovery, and look forward to hearing from you.

Respectfully yours,

Sir George Mallet,

Governor-General.

Cc: Councillor Ben Bousquet.

Time, however went by without any further news and Joy was beginning to become concerned that the bones would be left at Ilfracombe Museum indefinitely. In addition it must be stressed that a significant percentage of people were not happy that Ilfracombe was embroiled in controversy at all. Joy is the last person in the world who would wish to upset anyone, and yet as curator of the museum she was inadvertently in the front line. Then out of the blue she received a message signifying that Mark Horton was coming down to visit the museum, with a view to looking at the site in the cove.

§

Mark Horton arrived at the museum in company with Susan Giles from the Ethnography and Foreign Archaeology section of the Bristol Museum and Art Gallery. This department, it seemed, could offer conservation facilities. Their interest was compounded by the fact that Bristol was the destination of *The London* before it wrecked. They were in Ilfracombe to offer guidance to the North Devon District Council in order to resolve this difficult issue, and because Bristol University had shown great interest in the site. Importantly, the University had the expertise and facilities to study the bones under Dr Juliet Rogers and Dr Jonathan Musgrave, and to carry out an isotopic analysis under Dr Richard Evershed

At Rapparee Dr Horton asked me if I believed there were any more burials left to excavate. I told him that in my opinion there were, because the excavation I undertook did not explore the lower levels, and there was still lime showing in the strata in two places, which clearly indicated that it was undisturbed. From the cove we visited my house, and I took the ironwork out of the Rayburn oven, where I was drying it after removing the salts in the micro-pores of the metal by washing it in fresh distilled water for several weeks. This has the effect of stopping further corrosion. Both Dr Horton and Susan Giles were far from convinced that the iron work necessarily represented a fetter (see illustration on page 60) nevertheless a date was there and then arranged for a Bristol University-led excavation.

§

The Excavation In Rapparee Cove, Undertaken By Bristol University, In July 1997.

I was asked if I would make myself available to help dig the site in Rapparee Cove with the Bristol University archaeological team directed by Dr Horton and I readily agreed. On 2nd July the team confirmed that they were pleased that I would be present on the dig, and I was asked to bring my equipment over to the cove where the digging had already started. I had loaded my waterproof case with drawing and measuring gear, a camera, and my trusty camcorder.

I arrived at the cove by about 12 noon where Dr Horton and the team had already cleaned and trowelled back the left section of the site. We broke for lunch at 1pm and afterwards this section was trowelled down a few more inches. The first bone, a fragment of rib was found by 2pm.

Later in the afternoon, to the right of the location of this bone, were found some rib fragments. The worn angular sloping surface of the living rock, was formed in such a way that loose scree falling from above was naturally directed into the filled area where the bones were buried. However, the bones themselves did not fall from above (which was a point the excavation hoped to prove, or disprove), but probably originate from burials in the disturbed sloping bank that had been dug, when various walls were erected to retain and stabilise it at various times during the past.

Mark asked me to join in the trowelling on the far right side against the remaining standing wall section. We then all trowelled away from the foot of the existing bank towards the foot of the remaining wall base, which stood just clear of the concreted area that was covered with shingle washed up by the wave action of high tides. After this area was trowelled off clean, various colour changes could be seen, where the grey/blue shale, displaced yellow clay. A distinct line, 159mm wide, ran from the base of the bank directly towards the wall. This line feature was positioned about a third of the distance across the site, and was thought to represent the edge of a grave cut. Two bones were found within this area, the first by me, which was found just after 2pm The next was a large pelvis fragment which appeared to be from a male, judging by the size of the internal cavity. This bone was found at 3pm, and was positioned 1.7m into the site from the marker stone, in the remaining wall next to the base of the pillar which itself is 4.8m from the rock face on the right side of the site.

To the left of this was an area where beach gravel was spread, as if to form the narrow shape of a grave, with three rocks across the lower edge. However, the feature abruptly ended and its purpose became unclear when no bones were found in the gravel. Thus, the first day only produced displaced bones, none of which were articulated.

At 4.45pm we moved the large boulders that were covering the left section of the site where the sea had completely destroyed the wall to ground level. The boulders had to be removed in order to dig the site which was hidden below them. We moved the boulders just beyond the old wall line, to act as an edge to stop the spoil from sliding back into the site; which in this section was at the foot of the concrete ramp.

The strategy on the 3rd of July was to ascertain if the left half of the site had any more bones buried in it, because this section did not show any soil colouration to indicate a grave cutting. Thus, the plan was to quickly dig the section down, whilst keeping a close watch for any bones that may have been mixed with the shale. One of the women and I undertook this task, but found no bones this fill. However, by 12.45pm we did find a feature low down at the back, that was clearly running back into the bank. A large rock was sloping down the steep bank behind this feature, above which the slope had been trowelled off the previous day. The feature was composed of yellow clay about 1m wide, and 300mm deep, surrounded by a ginger coloured 'iron panning' band. The feature had a black elongated centre which may have been connected to the walled structure that could be seen amongst the bracken above, but we never fully investigated this. Just after 3pm we had dug the strata off to about 400mm depth in our section of the site, and Mark declared that it could safely be written off, because clearly it was not a burial level.

The right section of the site did still have bones buried in it and these were cleaned, and made ready for photographing, by the skilfully executed work performed by the experienced women excavators. The site was at last yielding the required evidence, and these particular bones appeared to be articulated. Also of interest is the fact that the newly found bones may have been the remaining lost parts of the bones and skull found by Peter Russell, and the fragments found by Jeanne and I prior to, and on the excavation performed on 22nd February 1997. Also these bones may have been connected with the location of the skulls mentioned in my interview with Paul Howard of Ilfracombe, on 26th February 1997. The possibility also existed that the child's skull fragments found on the 22nd February 1997, and identified by Dr Juliet Cross as being those of a child 4 & 8 years old, may have been the missing parts of some of the newly found fragments. We await the analysis of these bones for the answer.

The women had started to trowel into the yellow clay that was so prominent in the right section area, and the first bones unearthed on the 3rd July were ribs (group No.6), which were at the left end of this section (approximately the middle of the site). There was a lower arm bone in this group, buried just below the ribs, which were first exposed at 11.50am. The first of the vertebrae which included finger bones, were found about the same time as the previous group. At 12.30pm a lower arm bone and some toe bones were also uncovered, and by 12.50pm the women were picking, and meticulously clearing away clay from around the bones with small sharpened sticks. The next group, were found near to the standing wall at the far right end of the site; there were three skull fragments in this group at the base of an angular sloping boulder on which a skull may have been smashed, and thus these fragments ended up just below its slopes. These were being uncovered by 3.15pm and other skull fragments were found on the top slope of the same boulder, possibly part of the same smashed skull. The lower skull fragments were surrounded by a compacted black filled area, and the layer of black fill was surrounded by the yellow clay that covered this end of the site. These fragments were thought to represent parts of a newly discovered skull. By 3.50 pm, a hand water sprayer was deployed to clean off the bones before they were photographed. At this stage it began to look as if the bones were redeposited, but may have had something still holding them together originally, or perhaps the groups simply represented a convenient shovel full in the place where it landed. However, I don't think the spinal section had ever been removed from its original burial place. These matters may be clarified at a later date by a bone specialist. At 3.55pm Paula Gardner was plotting in the bones on the drawing, and by this time, the vertebrae and phalanges were showing very clearly after the water spray was used. By 4pm all the bones had been cleaned and photographed. The site was then covered over with a black polythene sheet to protect the remains overnight, and the tools were left under the same sheet in the deeper left half of the site.

The next morning, on the 4th of July I was first to arrive at the site. The group were staying at a nearby youth hostel and they arrived soon after. Laura and Mark started to survey the beach levels just after 11am. They started from the low water mark and worked their way back up to the site. This was done so that the bones could be levelled in on the drawings. At 11.15am the bones were freshened up yet again with the water spray, and by 1.00pm the bones and site, including the remaining stones in the wall were cleaned up for the final photograph. We waited for the sun to go behind a cloud, so that long shadows would not spoil the camera shot, but in the end we had to resort to holding up the black polythene sheet to shade the site. After the photos were finally taken the bones were removed and named as they were placed into labelled polythene bags. The site was finally back filled by 6.40pm with the help of Alison Mills and a friend. We then carried the equipment out of the cove and the site was declared finished.

§

Earlier that day the *North Devon Advertiser* reporter Geoff Staddon had arrived and took a photo of me, Ben Bousquet, and Mark Horton positioned behind the bones. Ben Bousquet had arrived with his wife at the site just before 1.00pm. At 2.40pm, Guy Harrop the photographer from the *North Devon Journal* arrived and took photos of Jo Avery and Laura Bassell in the process of clearing the debris from amongst the bones.

Jeanne and George Hardwick had visited the site on

3rd July and I had been glad to see them. We had discussed progress and talked of the first dig in which we had all actively taken part. Fortunately the weather had been favourable on the last three days of the Bristol University excavation, even if the first day had been wet and dreary. Now, the sun was shining at its best, making the site all the more pleasing to our visitors.

Various members of the public showed an interest in the new discoveries. We had a couple of regular local visitors, and Peter Russell and his girl- friend Lesley also called around to see us. This was the first time I had met Peter, although Lesley had helped on the original dig. Thus I was fortunate to get a group photograph which included Peter and Lesley, myself, and Dr Horton and also a group photo of the women from Bristol University. To me, this all helped to alleviate the sombre nature of the dig make the project both a success and a memorable experience.

The bones, including the group found during the February dig, were then taken back to Bristol University and a scientific strategy of study dated 12th March 1997, has been set out by Dr Mark Horton and reads as follows:

> What was the date of the bones, are they from the wreck of The London, and are they the remains of 40 or so prisoners, of Afro-Caribbean origin, who were drowned on The London, and who were buried, according to much later account, [sic] on the beach at Rapparee Bay.

Dr Horton's plan is broadly as follows (although I have necessarily shortened it in the interest of clarity). The intention is to use Radiocarbon dating – AMS – to eliminate any prehistoric, or medieval origin.

An Osteological investigation, which will include the teeth, will establish if they compare with European or Caribbean populations that are already known. The method is none destructive as far as the bones measurements are concerned.

Mitochondrial DNA analysis will be carried out in the hope of finding a common maternal ancestor, linking with a modern population; perhaps sampling Ilfracombe and St Lucia people.

There will also be an Isotopic analysis of the bone,

which it is hoped will give a geographical origin, to prove if the victims used African or Caribbean plants in their diets. (*Op.Cit. Bristol University*).

I sent a copy of the camcorder recording I made of the dig to Ben Bousquet which he required for the St Lucian Archives, and he sent me the following letter via Ilfracombe Museum:

Dear Pat.   *22 July 1997.*

It was so nice seeing you recently.
I have spoken to the High Commissioner who thinks very highly of the support which you have given us concerning the Saint Lucia .
Dr Horton has told me that without your help his dig would not be as successful as it was.
I thank you on behalf of the Saint Lucia people for the wonderful way you have assisted this whole episode. I also wish to thank you for the tape which I found very interesting.

My regards to your family.

Yours Sincerely,

Ben Bousquet.

9

African Reparation

I had been waiting for the next event in connection with Rapparee Cove with anticipation and great curiosity. This event was to take place on 1st August 1997, and I understand, annually from then on. It was an historic event, the likes of which has never been witnessed before in North Devon, and thus worth recording, in as much detail as possible. It was about people, pilgrimage, and respect for the dead

On 31st July Onatachi Wambu, who had originally attended the 2nd March press conference, rang me to ask if I would collect a public address system from a hire company in Braunton, which Roz and I did first thing the next morning. Onatachi had not arrived by 12-30pm, so Roz, myself and Maxine Jarrett who was staying with us took the system down to the cove car park after pinning a note on the door explaining what we had done.

After going on a slight detour owing to traffic problems, we arrived to find Onatachi and a large group of people talking to the press at the top end of the quay car-park. I got out and walked over to members of his group, whilst he was being interviewed and as soon as he saw us he came over. He introduced us to various friends including Spartacus R.

Spartacus R. passed out some leaflets advertising his name and explaining what he did, which is worth recording here because some idea can be gained about the intellectual level of the people who were present. Spartacus R is a wordsmith of the highest calibre, and has written *The Maat Mystery: in Search of the Missing Link*. Other books include *Religion and Spirituality*;

Violence and Power; *The Five Stages of the Healing Process*; *Population Control*; *Towards 2000; Leadership and Self-determination*. Spartacus R. came to prominence in the early 70s as the founder and driving force of the first internationally famous African Rock band, *Osibisa*, and recorded *Africa I See*. He owns the *Zara Music Records* label and has travelled the world playing to audiences in Africa, America, Australia, Europe, Japan. Musician, Poet, Author, Columnist, Talk show host, Human Rights Activist and Teacher. Spartacus has shared platforms with some of the world's most celebrated speakers, including Jesse Jackson who dubbed him 'The African'.

Spartacus R. has also written *Violation*, *The Human Value*, *Love and Life* and *Global Eyes*. He is also the editor and publisher of *Global Africa Pocket News* known as *GAP News*.

By the time we headed down into the cove it was just after 1.00pm. We followed the winding path around the corner, treading carefully as we descended the steps because the air was full of light drizzle and the steps were slightly slippery. Even so, the day stayed reasonably dry.

After our small group of people had arrived on the shingle, the cove quickly began to fill with a dispersed crowd in variety of colourful clothes. At the top of the steps a man in white robes was constructing a raised grave from stones and seaweed. I considered telling him about *The London*'s ballast, thinking perhaps some of the yellow stones ought to be used as part of any symbolic memorial. The man noticed me and looked curiously in my direction, and as I set off to find a piece of the ballast he followed me. As I picked up a small, round example of the ballast the man caught up with me and showed interest in what I was doing. Suddenly other people started to look for the yellow pebbles and quickly I was surrounded in a semicircle with my back to the sea. I began speaking and related the various accounts of the wreck of *The London*, and noticed that the man in the white robes now had a camera man with him and they were filming me. I was asked numerous questions from the people around me and answered as clearly as I could, though I am nervous on such public occasions. I told the stories, as various people questioned me on the subject of the history of the wreck. Then somebody asked who I was and I was embarrassed to think that I had not introduced myself as soon as I had started to speak. Maxine Jarrett told me later that even before I had spoken lots of the people were asking her, "Who *is* that man over there?"

There were many local people in the crowd, including a lady who had heard some people talking about the ceremony at the *Cart Linhay Heritage Centre* at Mortehoe. Also in the crowd was my wife Roz; Mike Edmonds, who is an Ilfracombe councillor, and Mrs Smiles, a very popular lady connected to New Labour who wanted to ask Bernie Grant about problems concerning the prospective closure of the cottage hospital at Lynton. Mrs Smiles, at one time, looked to be having a very enjoyable conversation with the Nigerian chief Amuleweye. There were various news reporters, including Steven Cape of the BBC; and Sharon Goble from Westcountry TV, who stayed with her team on the lofty cove balcony near the top of the steps, coming down later to watch from a built-up stage by the arched building, on the far side of the cove.

Steven Cape, who was aware that some delicacy was required during his filming approached me cautiously along with his camera man. Indeed one of the crowd demanded to know what he thought he was doing. He indicated that he would like to interview me lower down the cove at the water's edge. As a lot of the people in the cove were now filming and taking photographs I considered it must be OK and began to take just a few shots of my own.

I was then introduced to various preachers from different religious groups and countries. I found all of them, without exception to be keenly interested, polite pleasant and respectful. In addition having spent all of my life in North Devon I was naturally both flattered by their attention and fascinated by their various cultures. The tribal chief from Nigeria, who was dressed in full costume, was interviewed by Sharon Goble on the lofty cove balcony. Bernie Grant, who had arrived with the chief, was also interviewed. Some other colleagues of Mr Grant, Matesha Ababa, Iris, and Sharon Lawrence were walking on the cove shingle welcoming people warmly as the crowd grew larger.

At 3pm a hushed murmur greeted the arrival of a group of white robed African spiritualists known as *The Answer Anset Society*. They descended the steep steps in a long line resembling a slowly wavering ribbon, contrasting the grey rock background of the cove. This scene added to an irresistibly potent inner feeling of awe for all concerned as the cove was transformed into a panorama of colour set alive by the moving crowd. Small children in baby buggies completed the family atmosphere, and when everybody was safely gathered on the beach the ceremony began.

Four drums of various sizes with large brown and orange chequered designs commenced a rhythmic and enchanting beat. I turned and spoke to a preacher in a round flat-topped hat, who was holding his baby son in his arms, and he smiled as he explained various points relative to the ceremony. Then a man began chanting from up on the natural rock stage talking of his ancestors, with emphasis on such words as "misery" and "ocean."

I asked Bernie Grant if it were likely to offend anyone if I recorded the events on my camcorder and he assured it would not, "you are welcome here, as a guest."

The chanting continued with the words:

Mothers torn from children, husbands from wives, from sun up to sun down, and attempt annihilation, and generational trauma. We are here to remember and rattle the bones of the dead. Call on Toussaint and...... and those who came before, who sacrificed from every day sunrise, who kept the drums alive and the secrets of the ancestors. We remember our past, we are the warriors, leaders, builders.... to walk our path of freedom and determination. For drums and battles not yet fought. We are here, we remember the tradition of the ancestors..... like to begin with....

After this, the Chief came forward and an interpreter repeated his words. The crowd was facing the stage and listened intently as the libation began. It was incredible; a wonderful sight, sheltered as they were beneath a sea of umbrellas, as the light drizzle again fell. Dazzling gowns of orange, bright blue, turquoise; multicoloured shapes and sizes and various African style hats; everybody watching intently. It was indeed a sight never before seen in North Devon — A truly historic occasion. The chief began to speak:

Come forward from the highest councillor....

The interpreter repeated as the chief poured Nigerian Palm wine from a green labelled bottle and into a bowl:

I give honour to spirit of Etti. I give honour to men of the event and water of earth. I give honour to the children of the world and water of the earth. I give honour to the death of the ancestors, who died here many years ago. Today many give homage to Aran who knew Raston Jaffa. I give honour to remembrance of various peoples' names. I give honour to representatives Bernie Grant and others. We give respect and honour to various people. A day of joy and sadness. The day has become a remembrance and remembrance of us in the heavens. Today each person of African ancestral descent remember years uncertain tonight. Today it is said.... the ancestors and the inner eye. Let us honour our ancestors.

Nigerian Palm wine was then poured into the bowl and the chief continued:

The dead must depart up. We must attend the dead.

The audience applauded loudly as the chief finished, and as he walked back down the ramp he shook hands with Bernie Grant.

Next a young man sang a spiritual lament; a mourning song. The song was about "going home inside of me." As he finished singing the crowd chanted "amen."

At 3.20pm The white cloaked *African Spiritual Society* were next to sing. They numbered about 30 people and began with a plain chant after forming themselves into a sitting circle. The chant began softly and gradually increased both in volume and intensity. At the height of the volume they all rose to their feet, before lowering themselves into a bowed posture the chant continuing all the while. They were joined in an accompaniment by a man talking the story in rhythm to the group's chorus-like chant. His powerful, melodious voice could be heard effortlessly rising above saying:

In peacetime, may we live our lives.... our lives....

And the female members of the chorus increased in volume. The "live our lives" theme was repeated over and over again.:

> *Joy of life and ancient wisdoms. Let us not forget our ancestors, and the atrocities... survivors and power. Pour libation.... regarding the atrocities.... Peter M, who died. May we not forget those who died, the atrocities... Peter M, and Malcolm X, and Peter M, who I am describing today.... Peter M, Peter M, Peter M, Peter M.... and the great warriors, we salute all those men, may we honour them.*

The music was so potent and haunting that once heard it was never likely to be forgotten,. The group then finished some of them and, without shoes, went down and stood in the water with their backs to the sea. I was told they were thinking of the dead whilst doing this and that the dead would be in their dreams for three days.

At 3-40pm the church minister, with whom I was speaking earlier was now wearing a brightly coloured hat with a flat top and he began addressing the crowd. Next was a woman who spoke about the history and cruelty of slavery. At 4-30pm I headed back to the Lantern Centre to meet representatives of the District council, who were there to welcome Mr Grant.

§

Most TV stations carried the story of the ceremony at Rapparee Cove. The BBC began their report with the words: 'Today is *African Reparation* Day which is held in America and now in Britain.' They then reported how people from all over the country had travelled to the archaeological site in Rapparee Cove to partake in the event. The programme showed TV footage of myself showing Steven Cape the ironwork in April, and some of my recent video recordings of the July excavation, with the Bristol University team. Then Dr Mark Horton at the university talking about his proposals to test the bones scientifically.

Then Bernie Grant was interviewed saying, 'The cove symbolises the struggle for freedom.' Next Ben Bousquet, the councillor from St Lucia was interviewed. He talked of ascertaining absolutely that the bones from the cove were those of St Lucians. That if they were from the wreck of *The London* they were 'freemen' and not 'slaves'. He went on to say that the people of St Lucia want the remains of their heroic ancestors back on the island, to be buried in Heroes Park.

The commentator for the BBC concluded: "For the moment the secret of the identity of the bones found at Rapparee remains unsolved."

The BBC then cut to the studio where Linda Bellos was asked whether it were likely that those on board had been prisoners-of-war and not slaves. She replied flatly:

"They did not go to St Lucia on a Package Tour. They were taken there in chains. If the bones are from Africans, they are our ancestors."

A second news report later in the day, mentioned about the proposal for a permanent monument to be erected in the cove. The cameras then zoomed in on me standing on the rocks, as Steven Cape stated: "It is a poignant moment for the man that discovered the bones." He then asked what I thought of the event, and I said: "It's humbling, it's moving and it's long overdue. A sleeping element of North Devon's history, the history of them as well as us. It's awoken at last, and now they are going to pay homage to the dead, that is long overdue."

Next an elderly man dressed in black robes faced the TV cameras: "The Triangular Trade has left people scattered all over the world. We are here to remember our people. It is wonderful to be able to identify a particular part of the world, and have actual tangible evidence."

Then the Nigerian Chief was interviewed: "I remember our dead ones from all over the world." Around his neck he wore a type of purse embroidered with the legend: *amulewaye iledi doni ile ife*. I was told this was his name and his tribe's name, but I do not know this for sure.

Then Bernie Grant was focused on, saying: "People came down here today to reconcile, and ease some of the pain and suffering of enslavement."

The cameras had homed in on the drummers, as the first speaker was saying:

"To remember those dragged in life sapping dungeons. Peter M, Peter M, Peter M, Peter M, we live our lives, Altrouta, Altrouta, Altrouta, Altrouta, women still chained, countless millions died, we remember those

who died in this area. Those who died in services, we know what that means. The people who died in this area cry out for burial right. To recall and remember them. We will return in a few months time to remember them. If we have no past, we have no future."

On the 1st of August the chairman of North Devon District Council, councillor Edward Nightingale, invited Roz and myself to tea and biscuits at the Lantern Centre, Ilfracombe to mark the visit of Mr Grant and guests, at 3.30pm. It was a quiet meeting with the focus of attention concentrating on the idea of a new monument to honour those who had died in the wreck of *The London*.

§

The following day (2nd August 1997) we held the first conference, which was chaired by Bernie Grant, discussing the erection of the monument

A few days before, Alison Mills rang me to ask if I knew the time of arrival of any of the guests and at what time they were expected at the hall. I readily agreed to a suggestion by Alison that I help welcome people to the ceremony. I felt that Alison was more at ease with me since the issue concerning the temporary resting place of the bones had been resolved.

On arriving at the hall I was greeted by Alison, and she asked if I would be good enough to rush home and fetch my video recording of the second excavation which had been undertaken by the team from Bristol University. Excitedly, I ran all the way home to fetch it, returning quickly, if rather the worse for wear. Our guests were sitting anxiously, waiting to see the promised video and I was slightly horrified to remember, as the cassette whirred into play that the student element of the Bristol team, (while very professional excavators) had at the time been in high spirits.

Roz, had previously remarked that these antics had appeared a shade distasteful, and even disrespectful. I was now concerned that it might appear so to the people in the room. It really was only the natural high spirits of students which had occurred during the excavation (and actually, overall, was a serious and solemn occasion) but

111

could be seen as unnecessary prancing, and pratting about to the people who had just returned from a traumatic visit to the cove. In any case it was clear to see on the screen and Alison, ashen, discreetly turned it off and reverted to her slides.

Next a formal meeting began and Bernie Grant – as mutually agreed – became spokesman. He was concerned as he had expected some representatives of the St Lucian isles who had not, as yet, arrived. He then asked about the gold coins found in the cove. At this, Alison perked up and announced : "Pat Barrow found some."

I then told Bernie about the gold, and he asked me about the ballast from the ship, which is still present in the cove. This was important evidence according to Gosse's account of 1853 (see page 9) although Alison, in her own words was 'deeply cynical'. She tended to dismiss this evidence in her report, on the grounds that:

> *The prime motive to explain gravel – though yellow flint at Rapparee is common along N. Devon coast, often in concentrations and is not imported. Local opinion clearly associating black prisoners and jewels.*

I explained to the meeting that there had been a suggestion that Gosse's account may not be valid (at the time I was unaware of the importance of Gosse as a world-renowned Naturalist) but a document in the Public Records Office in London shows how a second ship called the *New Adventure* with a captain named Ingate, did indeed arrive at Ilfracombe at the same time as *The London* just as Gosse had suggested though it was not wrecked. I felt it was probable that Gosse had also got right the story of the ballast.

Alison then mentioned her theory that this 'ballast' was to be found all along the coast.

My reply to this was that I believed the yellow pebbles which appear in Rockham Bay and other places at low tide *are* different than those found in Rapparee Cove. I went on to clarify the point as I had carried out some research into the issue only recently. I stated that the pebbles in Rockham Bay and other places were deposited by glaciers in the *Anglian Period*, which was between 423-478 thousand years ago. It would appear that this was the only time when a glacier came far

Early 19th century painting by J Walter(s) depicting the wreck of 'The London' displayed in the Maritime Room of Ilfracombe Museum

*The Reverend John Mill Chanter MA, who was 51 years Vicar of Ilfracombe,
was born in the Parsonage at Hartland, Devon 25th March 1808*

bove : Coins belonging to Keith Harker, including a Portuguese 4000 reis minted in Brazil, ated 1724; a 2 escudo/ Doubloon, Spanish Colonial; a Portuguese 8 escudo dated 1725 and a rtuguese 8 escudo dated 1723.

Photo, courtesy of Mr Harker.

elow : P Barrow and K Harker coins including a James II gold guinea dated 1686

Above: *1689 coin found by the author*

Below: *Close view of the first gold coin found by the author on 14th January 1978*

Above: *Another selection of coins found by P Barrow and K Harker*

Below: *Rapparee Cove in 1978*

Photo courtesy Nick Pugsley of Ilfracombe

The author digging in 1984

Roz Barrow standing by the Chiswell's family grave

Above : *Rapparee Cove in 1984 when the wall was still complete*

Below : *Radius, ulna and scapula bones, excavated 22nd February 1997*

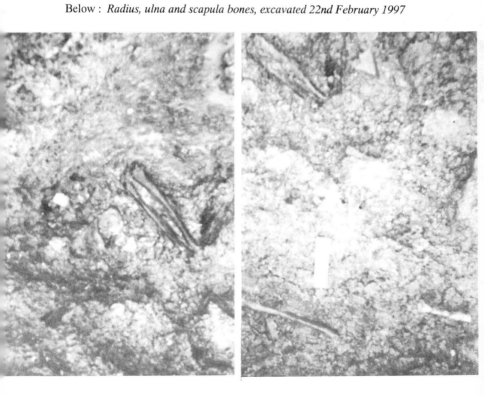

Trays of bones laid out in Broad Park Avenue Ilfracombe. The child's skull fragments are in the second tray up on the right. The Ironwork is in the bottom left tray

Above: *The author beside a tray of arm bones*

Below: *The site photographed by the author in 1997*

Above: *Some of the people who were present on 22nd February 1997. From left to right, they are Julie Parker, Roz Barrow, George Hardwick, Pat Barrow, and Richard Ashford*

Below: *Ben Bousquet, from St Lucia, Dr Mark Horton (Bristol University) and Pat Barrow*

Above : *The excavation team from Bristol University digging the site in July 1997*

Below : *Dr Mark Horton, Pat Barrow, Lesley and Peter Russell. Jo Avery is at bottom left*

Ilfracombe *from the Anchorage in the Range S. W. by S.*

BRISTOL CHANNEL

ILFRACOMBE

HARBOUR

SURVEYED BY LIEUT H M DENHAM R.N

A map of Ilfracombe Harbour and the Bristol Channel surveyed by Lieut. HM Denham RN
It is dated 1839

Above : *Rapparee Cove from above, August 1997*

Below: *An early 19th century view of Lantern Hill from Rapparee Cove*

Above: *The author discussing details of his research with Bernie Grant MP*

Below: *Mr Grant and the author at the conclusion of the first visit*

Above: *Mayor of Ilfracombe, Doug Ray with the High Commissioner of St Lucia, Aubrey Hart and the author at Ilfracombe Museum, 12th March 1997*

Below : *The site, stormwashed, March 1988*

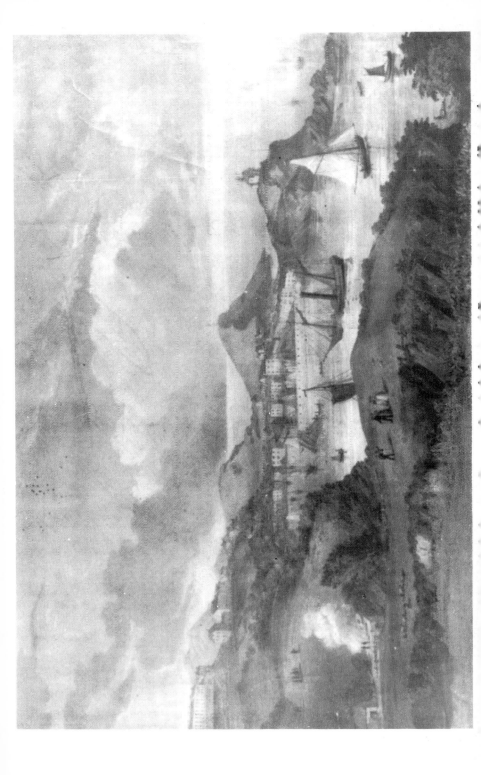

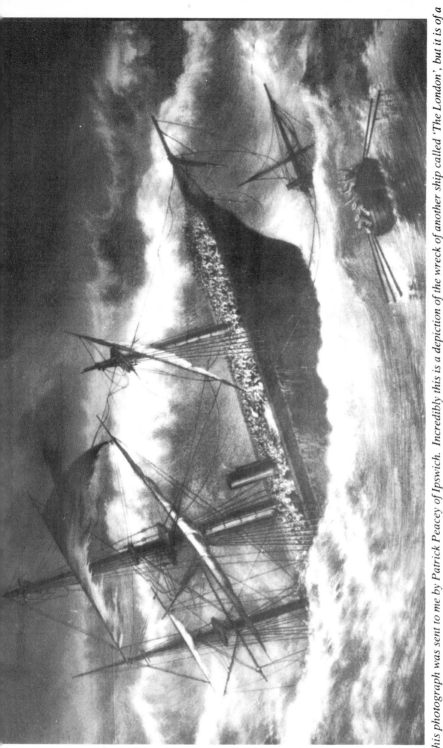

This photograph was sent to me by Patrick Peacey of Ipswich. Incredibly this is a depiction of the wreck of another ship called 'The London', but it is of a later period. The painting is entitled 'Loss of The London'

Above : *Rapparee Cove. High tide and gales 4th January 1998.*

Below : *Rapparee Cove. Calm 27th July 1997*

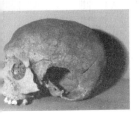

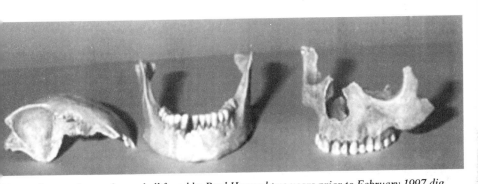

Above : *Lower picture shows skull found by Paul Howard two years prior to February 1997 dig*
The picture (top right) shows a section of the prised-open chain link

Below : *A member of the African Spiritualist Society builds a symbolic grave of stones*

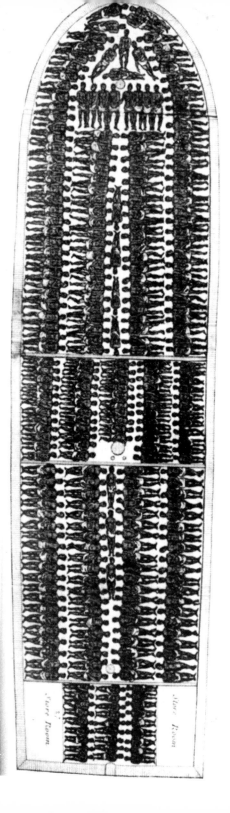

Graphic depiction of the conditions aboard an 18th century slave ship

The African Remembrance day banner

Above : *The Nigerian chief Amulewaye.in Rapparee Cove on 1st August 1997*

Below : *The white robed African Spiritualists*

above : Maxine Jarrett, Bernie Grant, Pat. Barrow & Matesha Ababa outside the Lantern

below : Roz Barrow, and visitor's child in the Lantern Centre, Ilfracombe   2nd August 1997

Ian Chambers and Leonard Hendrick, curator and deputy curator of Ilfracombe Museum

enough south (three ice-ages ago). It seemed to me that some people *wanted* the gravel at Rapparee not to have been from the wreck of *The London*. With hindsight, and now knowing who PH Gosse was, it is highly unlikely he would make such an assertion lightly. I firmly believe Gosse was right – this yellow gravel *is* unlike any other found around this coast.

Bernie Grant, then asked again for something to be done to protect the site. I must confess I have not noticed, since, any action to protect the site even though Mr Loates (referred to earlier) of North Devon District Council has described the site as sacred.

Mr Grant enquired whether the representatives from St Lucia were likely to attend the meeting as he had understood they would do so. Ayodla Kabaka stood up to announce that she was from St Lucia but was unaware if the official representatives had arrived in Ilfracombe. She offered to provide any DNA sampling that may be required to test the origin of the bones.

10

Further Developments

As events moved on evidence continued to come to light even as this book was being written and at some stage I knew I would have to call a halt and send the book to press. To date there has been no result announced by Bristol University of their scientific study of the bones, although almost a year has passed. It is necessary for me now to re-examine some of the historic accounts of the wreck in Rapparee Cove, as well as to relate new ones as they presented themselves.

Are the details recorded by P H Gosse, correct?

It was in 1970 that I saw my first ever record regarding the wreck of *The London*. It was in a book written by P H Gosse, (Op.Cit.).

Gosse wrote about *two wrecks* that occurred in Rapparee Cove, one of which was *The London*. All of Gosse's references to the wreck are interesting and to analyse them, four individual topics need to be discussed separately. The first topic is where Gosse writes of: *two transports returning from the West Indies...*

(1)
The London – Sunday evening 9th October 1796

The fact that Ilfracombe was visited by two transports can be verified, because the archives at Kew in London have the original *Ilfracombe Port Book* records, for 1796 (ADM1/ 2894, Log 76), with the following account for 8th October 1796:

> *'The "New Adventure", of London, a transport, James Ingate, master, from St Kitts with French prisoners and troops, arrived at this port, being forced up this channel by stress of weather, in a leaky condition.'*

This first ship which Gosse mentions is here *not* recorded as wrecked in Rapparee Cove. To describe a ship as 'arriving' at a port is rather different than recording it as having been wrecked – even if it were 'in a leaky condition'. Another report in the *Ilfracombe Port Book* dated 10th October 1796 gives an account of the second ship and is very different:

> *'Last evening "The London" of London, a transport, William Robinson, master, from St Kitts with French prisoners aboard, was unfortunately driven on shore at the entrance of this harbour, upwards of 40 persons drowned. The vessel was entirely lost.'*

It is interesting to note in Gosse's account where he writes: *'...while attempting to enter the harbour of Ilfracombe in stress of weather.'* The use here, of the words 'stress of weather' is more than coincidental as it is similarly used in the *Port Book* account: *'...by being forced up this channel by stress of weather.'* It is possible Gosse may have referred, himself, to the *Port Book*. I believe he simply misread the entry (the handwriting is atrocious and extemely difficult to decipher). He was, though, mistaken only to this extent and there is no reason to doubt any of his other evidence.

It is unlikely that locals at the time of Gosse's account (1853) would have forgotten whether or not such an event took place. After all we have the accounts of 1856 (only three years later) stating that old men who had witnessed the wreck of *The London*, were still living. In the *North Devon Journal* 1856, the correspondent writes:

> *'...before calling in the evidence of either of the many old men now living...'*

This is in direct connection with the inquisition regarding the wreck of *The London* which appeared in the *Illustrated London News*. Nowhere is there further mention of *The New Adventure*.

115

Did *The London* wreck at Rapparee Cove
And how many people perished?

Having, I believe, fairly established that *The London* was wrecked on that fateful night and that it had sailed from the Caribbean I must now try to prove that it was driven ashore at Rapparee. It is described in the *Ilfracombe Port Book*, as:

> *driven onshore at the entrance of this harbour...*

Is this the same location suggested by Gosse when he writes:

> *...driven on shore in this cove..?*

The London could easily have been washed right into Rapparee Cove in that storm. One only has to look in the cove when tidal conditions are suitable, to see just how full of water it gets there. Since *The London* is recorded in the National Maritime Museum as drawing 15 feet of water when fully laden, it becomes more apparent that she *could easily* have washed right in.

John Chiswell tells the correspondent in the 1856 inquisition, that:

> *...she [The London] drifted in the storm, onto the Rapparee rocks, and there perished.*

This could, however, refer to the outer rocks, because a manuscript about the wreck of *The London* in the National Maritime Museum Library states:

> '*...in coming for this harbour, a heavy squall took & forced her upon the rocks; the Vessel went to pieces before day light.*'

If these rocks were at the entrance to the cove, then perhaps broken pieces of the wreckage were washed into Rapparee by the force of the waves. Indeed, a clear impression is given here that it was upon the *outer rocks* of the cove that *The London* met her end. This is also indicated in a statement, in connection with the bodies of the dead (in the 1856 account). The statement reads:

> '*...as they were washed in, not all at once.*'

This outer location for the wreck is also near the entrance to the harbour. I believe the ship would be likely to break up gradually releasing more bodies to be washed up on Rapparee. It *did* gradually break up, according to the account in the Maritime Museum and bodies were gradually washed in on Rapparee.

John Chiswell – who was one of the witnesses still living according to the *North Devon Journal* of 1856 – stated how he found everybody using all the means in their power to save as many of the passengers and crew as possible and that:

> '*Many of the coloured people on board, as well as others, were saved.*'

The correspondent of the *North Devon Journal* (1856) also mentions that:

> '*...the number of coloured people in the hold of the vessel is considered by this witness to have been about sixty. It was impossible to get at them and they were all, as stated in the Register, drowned in the wreck. Many others also perished, and as they were washed in, not all at once, their bodies were buried deep in the sand.*'

In the Annual Register for 1796, it is stated that:

> '*The London, from St Kitts, had on board a considerable number of blacks (French prisoners)...*'

The letter from Richard Allard, Governor of Stapleton Prison, asking for a boat to be hired to transport the survivors back to Stapleton Prison in Bristol, does not specifically mention the name of the wreck from which they came. I believe it can be safely asserted that it was *The London*.

(3)
The Gold Coins

The third subject mentioned by Gosse, is that of the gold coins. Gosse wrote:

> '*... and for years after the sad event the people of the town used to find gold coins and jewels among the shingle at low-tide.*'

There obviously was treasure on *The London* which is verified by the 1856 account, where it states:

...as well as can be now ascertained, the valuables on board were contained in five boxes - there were specie, in doubloons, dollars, etc. - one of which was lost in transit from the ship, and was no doubt broken up at the bottom of the sea, as dollars and doubloons continued to be found in the sand years after the ship was lost.

(4)
The Yellow Ballast

It has been suggested that the yellow flint at Rapparee Cove is common along North Devon, often in concentration, and is not imported (see page 112 where this is discussed in detail). Concentrations of the so called flint can indeed be seen at low tide in Rockham Bay. However, on recent closer examination I have found that the flint can be seen to be more rounded and generally different in colour and texture.

It must be remembered that Gosse was writing about *rambles* on the North Devon coast, and since the different type of yellow flint at Rockham is clearly a feature of the North Devon coast, and more abundant for all to see in places other than Rapparee Cove,— why should Gosse single out its presence at this location, and in connection with a shipwreck? This ballast he states:

'remains to bear witness of this shipwreck, and to identify the spot where it took place,'

In the *Transactions of the Devonshire Association* (1879 Vol XI) the respected North Devon Geologist Townsend M Hall concurs with Gosse, regarding 'yellow flint' at Rapparee, which he describes while discussing the geology of the North Devon coast.

In conclusion it is apparent that Gosse did know that *The London* sank in Rapparee Cove and there *were* people still living at that time who knew about the wreck. Those same people knew approximately how many people died in the wreck — an exact number eludes all records that I could find. The coins found in the cove in 1978 confirm that there were indeed, gold and silver coins present. The unworn condition of the coins also indicate that they had not moved far from where they were originally lost, and according to Gosse nor had the ballast from the wreck. These facts appear to confirm that the wreck did take place in or on the outer rocks of the cove as Gosse implied, before being washed further in by the tide.

§

When I called in at the offices of my publishers to hand over the first draft of this manuscript to my editor, Edward Gaskell, we discussed the events portrayed in Gosse's book. Edward assured me that Gosse was an important naturalist, and remembered that a well known author he knew had studied the life of Gosse with a view to a possible biography. Edward made some telephone calls and within fifteen minutes a fax was received confirming that Gosse was one of the most distinguished Naturalists of his day:

Palaeontologist, zoologist and oceanographer; early work in Canada and United States; published works include Introduction to Zoology, Birds of Jamaica, Naturalist's Sojourn in Jamaica, A Naturalist's Rambles on the North Devon Coast, A Manual of Marine Zoology, Actinolgia Britannica, and The Romance of Natural History. He was elected Fellow of the Royal Society in 1856, and was 'famous for the accuracy of his observation' and was sent to Jamaica by the British Museum. As a close friend of Darwin – while at the same time holding an intense, near-Quaker view of religion – the difficulties of reconciling emerging Darwinian science with the Old Testament account of Creation were in turn to create for Gosse the maddening dilemma faced and debated so hotly even today. He was the father of Edmund Gosse.

It can hardly be argued, then, that Gosse would be an unreliable source.

§

Are the 1856, and Later Reports About the Wreck of the London Likely to be Accurate?

The 1856 reports first appeared in the *Illustrated London News* and comprise of a series of letters (see page 31). The aim of this analysis is to try to break down the claims and counter claims of those involved in the correspondence in order to try to ascertain the accuracy of the details given.

The original contributor, who signed himself 'V' mentioned in an authoritative manner:

> ...at the north-east angle of this cove, just out of the reach of the flood tides and scarcely below the surface of the earth, are an immense number of human bones, the bodies appearing to been thrown there indiscriminately, not buried.

This location appears to be accurate because a receding flood tide at 8.13am on 12th March 1997 (which had been as high as 10.3m the previous day) was 9.9m high when a camcorder film showed the waves just washing the foot of the partly demolished site wall. Although I believe we can safely say that many skeletal remains were in evidence at this location in 1856 it is still not proven that such remains are from the wreck of *The London*. Therefore we must turn to the response to this letter which was sent by someone signing themselves N.V. (possibly Nathaniel Vye). This states:

> It is well known to many old men now living that about 60 years ago a vessel manned by blacks ran ashore, and that the then best families in the town being nothing but wreckers and smugglers, murdered the crew and buried the bodies on the beach, and then plundered the vessel of a very valuable cargo, consisting of ivory, doubloons, jewels etc. Many near descendants of the actual wreckers still reside here, and rank among the most respectable of the inhabitants.

Of course this letter would infuriate many of the local people in Ilfracombe. However, it is also clear that N.V of Ilfracombe knew something of the history of the remains in Rapparee Cove as he refers to 'many old men now living,' indicating that stories in connection with the wreck were at that time still being told – probably fuelled by the occasional discoveries of gold coins. It is unlikely that these people would forget the name of the wreck from where they came.

A correspondent for the *North Devon Journal* next takes up the challenge of writing to the *Illustrated London News* in a bid to defend the honour of the local inhabitants. He quotes *The Annual Register* for 1796:

October 16th

This evening a very melancholy accident occurred at Ilfracombe. A ship called the 'The London' from St Kitts, having on board a considerable number of blacks (French prisoners) was driven on the rocks near the entrance of the pier during a violent gale of wind, by which about 50 of the prisoners were drowned. Those who got on shore exhibited a most wretched spectacle, and the scene altogether was too shocking for description. The wind was blowing directly fair for the harbour.

These are the actual words that are printed in *The Annual Register*, and I have verified this by finding an original copy of this. The correspondent then quotes the evidence of a local man (one of the old men still living). He was John Chiswell who had been a young Pilot at the time of the wreck, and was said to have been personally involved in assisting the sufferers, and had witnessed the dreadful calamity. (see page 35)

There is some verification for these accounts in the *Sherborne Mercury*, which states:

In the evening, a melancholy accident happened at Ilfracombe, a ship called 'The London'....

Thus the wreck of *The London* is established as having happened that fateful evening. The *Ilfracombe Customs Book* dated 10th October 1796 clearly records the wreck, and uses the words: 'last evening' which clearly establishes both the date (Sunday 9th October 1796) and the time of day.

A second account states:

the inhabitants who were busily removing the dead bodies to the out-houses of the Britannia Hotel...

John Chiswell's account (a living witness), states:

many of the coloured people on board, as well as others were saved, and for them a shelter was speedily found in a large stable near the quay [undoubtedly that of the Britannia Hotel], *which was fitted up, as well as circumstances would allow, for their comfort..... the number of coloured prisoners in the hold of the vessel is considered to have been about 60, and it was impossible to get at them as they were all drowned in the wreck.*

The next piece of John Chiswells evidence appears in the 1856 *North Devon Journal* article, stating:

According to our venerable witness, everything that could be saved was duly accounted for to those whom it concerned. As well as can be now ascertained, the valuables on board were contained in five boxes-there was specie, in doubloons, dollars, etc.- one of which was lost in transit from the ship.'

A Spanish quarter dollar (Pillar Dollar) was found in the cove in 1978 by Brian Bradshaw and was badly corroded, but the date 1784 could clearly be seen. Thus we have direct evidence that the coinage known as 'dollars' were not only recorded as having been lost in the cove in connection with the wreck of *The London*, but actually found there in recent times.

In the Green Book in Ilfracombe Museum there is the following account:

as the waves moved the sand on the beach, heaps of shining coins in gold met the sight of the astonished inhabitants, who were busily removing the dead bodies. The sight was a wondrous and not an unwelcome one. Eagerly they rushed to the treasure.

Other coins found recently such as the Portuguese gold coins were almost certainly booty from the second battle of the Saints (not the group of islands called *Les Saintes*), because an English gold guinea dated 1686 was found mixed with two of the Portuguese gold coins (dated 1689 & 1720, (see, *North Devon's Gold*, by P H Barrow, in Barnstaple Athenaeum), and these may appear rather old in connection with the 1796 battle for the islands; but also found near these coins was a

French Demi-em dated 1683 that was minted at Rennes.

Clearly older coinage was still in use and mixed in with other coins – such as the French coin, which itself is likely to have been a coin captured at the battle of the Saints and was being sent back mixed with other coinage from the Islands. And since no other ship has been recorded as having lost any treasure in Rapparee Cove then *The London* is clearly the only possible source.

One possible answer as to the question of why the bodies were not given a Christian burial is suggested in the Green Book as follows:

The cry is raised by some one. Stop! First bury the dead. They hesitated, but the inward voice of conscience re-echoed the mandate, and they returned to their sad work, and the bodies were hastily buried in the hill-side, this being the most convenient spot near at hand.

What actually happened we will probably never know.

We can return to 'V', in the *Illustrated London News*, (January 19th 1856) for supporting evidence:

'In the north-east angle of this cove, just out of reach of the flood tides, and scarcely below the surface of the earth, are an immense number of human bone, the bodies appearing to [have] been thrown there indiscriminately, not buried.

The writer of the stories in the Green Book (*Old Times in the Westcountry*) was recording what other people had told of, and the author may have kept these anecdotes for some years before they were published, because John Chiswell was dead nine years before this book was printed. Incidentally, he died on 22nd February which is exactly the same day my first excavation began.

There are also some other facts that should be included regarding the bones. These came from John Penny in a letter dated 24th February 1997; who is a local historian from Bristol. He has done a considerable amount of research regarding the Admiralty Prison at Stapleton, Bristol. He wrote that in 1796:

some of the 4000 West Indian prisoners taken by Lord Abercromby, among whom were 30 to 40 French Creole officers, were imprisoned in Stapleton.

He also wrote that during epidemics at the prison, the bodies were placed in piles (with white lime and canvas only), and head to foot, to save space:

three groups of skeletons buried in this way have been found.

It should be noted here that the bones found in Rapparee Cove had large nodules of lime mixed with them, of which samples can be seen in Ilfracombe Museum.

Thus it may have been standard practice to bury prisoners-of-war in this way, in that period. The account mentioning the bodies at Rapparee being 'denied Christian burial' (*Transactions of the Devonshire Association*, 1879, vol. X1, P.167), were written by Mrs Slade-King (see page 12) who at the time was a well respected local historian.

There is also the actual eye witness account quoted in the Green Book which should not be overlooked, especially when other details have been shown to have a high degree of plausibility and similarity with other accounts.

These similarities in the previous accounts, and other various accounts of the wreck of *The London* are unlikely to be fabrications, because the modern evidence represented by the recent finds in the cove, in the form of the treasure and the bones of the dead, back up parts of the original statements by 'V', and parts of the accusation letter by 'NV' and other witnessed accounts mentioned in the records. Thus the story of the wreck of *The London* has more evidence to back it up than the unlikely case put for other wrecks, where no bones and no treasure are mentioned at all.

Thus in my opinion the bones buried in the north east angle of the cove, have to be those of the black freedom fighters drowned in the wreck of *The London*.

Shortly after the August visit to Ilfracombe by representatives of the *African Reparation Movement* I had received a telephone call from Jeanne at Ilfracombe Museum to say that she had found some new information. While conducting some (unrelated) research for Vic. Thompson – a popular figure in Ilfracombe who gives interesting and varied talks on local subjects – Jeanne came across a black cloth bound, loose-leaf book entitled *Mervyn Palmer's Note Book*. Mr Palmer was the first curator of Ilfracombe Museum, and in his book, turning to page 40, Joy found the following entries:

...Rapparree [sic] under Hillsborough. An African prince and his attendants are supposed to have been on board, how the[y] came to be off this coast is not told, anyway all hands were lost; and from time to time Negro skulls have been picked up about Hillsborough & the Quay & strange coins in the harbour mud. The people who flocked from far & near having heard of the news of a wreck, like so many love birds, are supposed to have picked up beautiful things in precious metals of strange foreign workmanship. That there was much money on this strange craft & that the people did much as they liked with it is proved by the following anecdote

[MGP abbreviates it]. A man who ran down to the wreck took some of his mother's dough to eat on the way. He picked up the "dollars" & put them in his pocket. The dough began to rise & brought the dollars with it out of his pocket. He was known as "Dollars & Dough" ever after. end of extract- See also the first of these notes re a SLAVER, told by "grandfather." P. 1 & P. 57. END of EXTRACTS from "WANDERINGS IN NORTH DEVON."

P. 57 records the following:

WRECKS at RAPPAREE.... Here at the commencement of the last war. [?which? MGP] two transports laden with black prisoners from the French West Indies were driven on shore & wrecked. Many lives were lost. Gold and jewels were long afterwards washed about among the shingle in the cove; and a few years ago several SKULLS [sic] were disinterred at the foot of the cliffs, two of which are now preserved in the COMMITTEE ROOM OF THE BOARD OF HEALTH in the town. A line of yellow gravel, between high and low water marks, may still be observed & and it is said to be the remains of the ballast of the unfortunate vessels.

The exact date at which the skulls noted by Mervyn Palmer as having been at one time preserved in the committee rooms of the *Board of Health* is not recorded, but can be safely said to have been in the 19th century. The account strikes a chord with that of Gosse, in his book dated 1853, and we know that the local *Board of Health* was formed in 1851 (Lamplugh, L.1984, p.65), and changed over to *Ilfracombe Urban District Council* in 1894 (ibid.), and that the *French Revolutionary Wars* took place between 1793 and 1815; and that the wreck of *The London* took place in 1796. The reference to 'the commencement of the last war,' undoubtedly refers to these wars, though it is surprising that Palmer queried it. In any event the date at which the skulls were on display has to be between 1851 and 1894. It is beyond doubt that the writer was referring to the remains of the bodies drowned during the wreck of *The London*.

Between 1851 and 1894, the skulls would still have been firm enough to move around. It is also interesting to note that the actual location claimed as the spot where the skulls were found is described as 'at the foot of the cliffs'. This is the same place where recent excavations have uncovered many more skeletal remains

There have certainly been many instances of gold coins found in the cove by various people even recently, such as in 1978. These coins – British, Colonial Spanish and Portuguese – were found together with French and other coins and jewellery. A Spanish quarter dollar gives us a terminus *post quem* on, or after 1784, for the loss of the coins, because it was the latest dated coin in the group recently found.

Thus, the coins mentioned in the records are verified by the modern evidence which confirms that there were indeed gold and silver coins in the cove, and these clearly fit the description of doubloons and dollars, which are recorded in evidence relating to the wreck of *The London.*

§

Shortly after discovering *Mervyn Palmer's Notebook* what appears to be an uncorrected proof of another book (which does not seem ever to have been officially published) was unearthed. Grandly entitled: *Wanderings in North Devon: Being Records and Reminiscences in the life of John Mill Chanter MA Oxon, 51 years Vicar of Ilfracombe*, it was printed by Twiss & Son, The High Street Ilfracombe in 1887. Turning to page 69 I found

the source of some of *Mervyn Palmer's Notebook* references. As Mr Palmer had copied verbatim parts of the
Reverend Chanter's records some of the section below is
necessarily repeated. However, as the author was so very
well respected in Ilfracombe, anything he had to say
concerning shipwrecks and in particular the events at
Rapparee deserve quoting in full :

*In old days the evil practice of "wrecking" was carried
on to a terrible extent all along the coast. One method
of enticing vessels ashore, was to place lights in
different spots along the cliffs. If the vessel was a
foreigner, or without pilot, it would often make for the
light, the crew thinking it was placed there to guide
them in. The 'William Wilberforce', which was wrecked
at Lee, gives a terrible instance of the villainy of which
the "wreckers" were capable. One Sunday night when
the people were in Church, and a gale from the north-
west was raging wildly round its walls, and at times
quite drowning the voice of the preacher, the shrill
note of a whistle was heard outside the door; the
startled congregation gazed at each other, and the
Coast Guards hurriedly rose and left the church. Mr
Cockbourn, their captain, was waiting for them
outside; there was a brig ashore at Lee, and they must
hurry there at once and see what could be done. But
nothing could be done, for the crew were all drowned,
seven lives altogether. The vessel was a timberman
from America and was supposed to have been wilfully
lured ashore by a man called Q., who had tied a
lantern on to his donkey's tail to make it appear to the
helmsman that he was perfectly free from the rocks
with plenty of sea-room. The action of the donkey on
the beach caused the lantern to move up and down,
just as a shiplight would by the action of the waves,
so causing the poor creatures to think there were
vessels anchored between them and the shore. The
seven sailors were buried in one grave, and a stone
raised to their memory.*
*About 80 years ago (but the date is vague) a ship ran
ashore at Rapparee under Hillsborough. An African
prince and his attendants are supposed to have been
on board; how they came to be off this coast is not
told, anyway all hands were lost; and from time to*

time negro skulls have been picked up about Hillsborough and the Quay, and strange coins in the harbour mud. The people who flocked from far and near at the news of the wreck, like so many evil birds, are supposed to have picked up beautiful things in precious metals, of strange foreign workmanship. That there was much money on board this strange craft, and that the people did much as they liked with it, is proved by the following anecdote:

"A woman had made some dough and placed it in a pan in the kitchen, where her son was sitting over the fire; he suddenly heard news of the wreck, and jumped up in haste to get his share of the plunder. But he was very hungry, and had been waiting for his meal some time, but how could he stay to get a slice of bread, when others might be making off with the best of the plunder? His hungry eyes alighted on the pan of newly made dough, and hastily filling his pockets, off he ran eating as he went. On the beach amongst others he found some dollars, which he put into his pocket. On his homeward way through the street, the dough began to work and raising itself out of the pocket carried the dollars with it. The joke was considered such a good one amongst the natives that the unfortunate youth bore the nickname "dollars and dough" to his dying day."

It seems very interesting that Mervyn Palmer should so faithfully quote the Reverend Chanter until he reaches the passage 'like so many evil birds...' — there, either by sleight of hand or unfortunate error the words become 'like so many love birds...'.

We will probably never know to whom the 'African Prince' mentioned refers. However, the complicated nature of the French Revolutionary Wars in the Caribbean and the intermittent – yet ultimately successful – insurrections of the black population against both French and British oppression brought forward (as in all wars) great leaders. Without doubt one of the greatest of these (and now considered one of the greatest fighters for black freedom in history) came to the fore at this time and his name was Toussaint l'Ouverture. He was born a slave on a French owned plantation in Haiti in 1743 and his father (who had been brought from Africa

128

CONTENTS

CHAPTER I.

CHAPTER 2.

129

to be enslaved) was the 2nd son of Gaou-Guinou, King of a powerful African tribe. It is possible, therefore, that amongst the black people who were on board *The London* that there would have been a leader, or leaders, at least one of whom would have been descended from the Chief of an African tribe. How the Reverend Chanter would have known this, or from where he heard the rumour, it is difficult to speculate. Still, it has a ring of truth about it – more especially as he obviously did not know at the time any other details of the ship, where it was from or its destination.

Two black Generals are mentioned in an account in the *Sherborne Mercury* (dated 4th October 1796) who were transported in the 103 ships in *The Ganges* convoy. The *New Adventure* was also part of that convoy, as was *The London*. A copy of part of this account is highly enlightening especially as it was written prior to the wreck taking place. It must be remembered that *The London* and *The New Adventure* have been described elsewhere as 'stragglers' and had arrived at the Bristol Channel some days behind the main convoy:

The homeward bound West- India fleet is safe arrived at Crookhaven without loss of a single ship under convoy of the Ganges, of 74 guns, consisting of 103 vessels. Some parted on their passage, bound for Liverpool. &c. the remainder, about 70, put into Crookhaven. They left the West Indies on the 27th of July and they have brought home about 3000 prisoners, the most of which are blacks, with two black Generals.

Another article is headed:

WHITEHALL June 18th

DESPATCHES, of which the following are copies have been received at the office of the Right Honourable Henry Dundas from Sir Ralph Abercromby, KB Commander in Chief of his Majesty's forces in the West Indies.

Head Quarters St Lucia May 2, 1796
SIR,
On 2nd April the fleet with the troops destined for the attack of St Lucia sailed from Carlisle Bay, and anchored on the evening of the 23rd in Marin Bay, Martinique, Admiral Sir John Laforey still

130

and good-will.   I am, &c.

RA. ABERCROMBY.

[Here follow the articles of capitulation, agreed to upon the 11th of June, on which day St. Vincent's capitulated. By those the garrison agreed to surrender as prisoners of war; the Negroes, &c. are to return to their respective proprietors; those who have been guilty of murder or of burning houses or estates, are to be subject to the judgment of the laws of the land; and the garrison is to march out with all the honours of war. These articles are signed, on the part of the British, by Sir Ralph Abercrombie and Captain Wolley; and on the part of the French by Ch. Sugue, Administrator; Bouny, Commandant en Second; D. Victor, Aid de Camp; and G. Audibert, Com. Del.

They found at New Vigie some brass ordnance, which are in general unserviceable; a quantity of shot and shells, 4000 musket balls, 1000 musket flints; and some other articles; and at Mounts Young and William sundry pieces of unserviceable brass ordnance, 24 fuzes, and some shot and shells.]

Return of the killed and wounded of his Majesty's Forces in the Attack of the Vigie, and adjacent Posts. St. Vincent's, June 10, 1796.

Total.—1 Captain, 1 Ensign, 4 serjeants, 1 drummer, 34 rank and file, killed; 1 Major, 5 Captains, Lieutenants, 1 Ensign, 15 serjeants, 6 drummers, rank and file, wounded.

Officers killed and wounded.

Captains Johnston and M'Lean, killed. Ensign Johnston, killed. Volunteer Gordon, wounded, since dead. Captains Douglas, Wharton, Elrington, and Ross, wounded. Majors De Lereal and Crosby, wounded. Lieutenants O'Donoghue, George Frazer, and Thirion, wounded. Ensign Rec, and Volunteers Clayton and Love, wounded.

SIR,   St. Vincent's, June 22.

[By
the Fre
or Dug
and Da
be trea
with th
public
faithfu

Return
woun
the
Tota
tain, 3
N.
wound

Extra
jesty'
King
S
I. H
my or
Abercr
the sea
Gen
of the
Otway
Hebe,
landing
pily ef
Since
from
Genera
made a
by Fed
the who

retaining the command. On the 24th Sir John resigned the command to Rear Admiral Sir Hugh C. Christian, KB and on the evening of the 26th we sailed for St Lucia. The disposition of the landing was arranged in the following manner. Major-General Campbell was ordered to disembark with 1700 men at Langueville's Bay, which he accordingly effected without opposition, except some shots fired from Pigeon Island.

In the morning of the 27th he advanced to Choc Bay. As soon as the head of the column began to appear, the center division of the army disembarked near the village of Choc, upon which about 500 men, who had faintly opposed Major-General Campbell on his march retired from Angler's plantation to Morne Chabor. This Morne is one of the most commanding posts in the neighbourhood of Morne Fortune, and as it was absolutely necessary to occupy it to be able to invest Morne Fortune, on the North side, two detachments from the army, under the command of Brigadier General Moore and Brigadier General Hope, were ordered to march that evening to attack it on two different sides.

From miscalculation of time, arising from the information of Guides, Brigadier-General Moore's division fell in with the advanced picquet of the enemy an hour and a half earlier than was expected. Finding that his march was discovered, and that it was impossible to halt the troops, who, from the narrowness of the path were obliged to march in single files, the Brigadier instantly decided to risk the attack with his own division, in which he was well seconded by the spirit of the troops who formed with all the expedition which the ground would omit of, and after a considerable resistance carried the post. Brigadier-General Moore speaks handsomely of the behaviour of the troops. From forty or fifty of the enemy were found killed, and [unreadable] of arms, with some ammunition, taken. The next day Brigadier-General Moore occupied Morne Duchaffaux, in the rear of Morne Fortune.

The division under the Command of Major-General Morshead, are now in possession of the Bar of the Grand Cul de Sac, and invest Morne Fortune on the South side.

Yesterday the enemy attacked the advanced post of

the grenadiers, who are commanded by Lieutenant Colonel MacDonald of the 55th regiment, but were repelled with considerable loss, though we had several officers wounded and forty or fifty men killed. The only Officer killed was Captain Kerr of the York Rangers, the rest are slightly wounded among whom is Major Napier.

RA ABERCROMBY

Another article headed *'From the London Gazette Extraordinary'* reads as follows:

St Vincent's June 21, 1796

SIR

Brigadier General Moore informs me in a letter from 18th June that everything remained quiet and I have every reason to hope that the measures he has adopted will tend to insure tranquillity as far as it depends upon him.

The embarkation of the artillery and troops destined to act in St Vincent and Grenada necessarily employed some days, and at the moment the weather proved particularly unfavourable. The whole, however, was embarked and ready to sail on the 3rd of June. The St Vincent division was ordered to rendezvous at Kingston Bay and that for Grenada at Cariacou, one of the Grenadines. While the troops were assembling at the rendezvous Major General Nicholls met me at Cariacou where the operations for Grenada were settled. On the 7th instant I returned to St Vincent and on the 8th in the evening the troops disembarked. The following day they marched in one column by the right as far as Stubbs, about eight miles from Kingston; each division halted that evening opposite to their respective point of attack. On the 10th in the morning the enemy's flank was turned. Two twelve pounders, two six pounders, and two howitzers were advanced with considerable difficulty within six hundred yards of the enemy's works; but not withstanding our efforts to drive the enemy from their post on the Old Vigie by means of a well-served artillery, they maintained themselves from seven in the morning until two in the afternoon. Major General Morhead had very handsomely early in the day offered to carry the redoubt by assault, but being willing to spare the lives of the troops, and observing that the part of the line which he commanded laboured under disadvantage, the assault was deferred for decline of the day rendered it absolutely necessary.

General Sir Ralph Abercromby.

From Major-General Hunter's division, on the night a part of Lewenstein's corps, and two companies of the 42nd regiment, with some island rangers, availed themselves of the profile of the hill, and lodged themselves within a very short distance of the fort. At two o'clock the two remaining companies of the 42nd regiment from Major-General Hunter's column, and the buffs, supported by the York Rangers from Major General Morhead's, were ordered to the attack. The enemy unable to withstand the ardour retired from their first, second, and third redoubts, but rallied round the New Vigie, their principle post. They were now fully in our power, as Brigadier General Knox had cut off their communication with the Charib country, and Lieutenant Colonel Dickens.... who had been previously ordered to make a diversion with the remains of his own and the West India regiment upon their right, where the Charibs were posted, had succeeded beyond expectation having forced the Charibs to retire and taken their post. The enemy, therefore, in the New Vigie, desired to capitulate which was granted.

The number of prisoners about 700. At the first of the attack, the Charibs, and, towards the close of it near 200 of the insurgents of the island made their escape into the woods. Lieutenant Colonel Spencer, with 600 men was immediately detached to Mount Young, and Lieutenant Colonel Gower with 300 men embarked to go by sea to Owia..[unreadable] but being unable to land on account of the surf, he has returned, the troops have been disembarked , and he has marched through the Charib country.

Signed   RA Abercromby

134

[Hereupon follow the articles of capitulation, agreed to upon the 11th of June, on which day St Vincent's capitulated. By these the garrison agreed to surrender as prisoners-of-war; the Negroes &c. are to return to their respective proprietors; those who have been guilty of murder or of burning houses or estates are to be subject to the judgement of the law of the land; and the garrison is to march out with all the honours of war. These articles are signed, on the part of the British, by Sir Ralph Abercromby and Captain Wolley; and on the part of the French by CH. Sugue, Administrator; Bouny, Commandant en Second; D Victor, Aid de Camp; and G Audibert, Com. Del.

They found at New Vigie some brass ordnance, which are in general unserviceable; a quantity of shot and shells; 4000 musket balls; 1000 musket flints; and some other articles; and at Mounts Young and William sundry pieces of unserviceable brass ordnance, 241 fuzes, and some shot and shells.

11

In Summary

The Revolutionary Wars broke out in 1793, and on March 26th of that year Sir Ralph Abercromby left the docks of Spithead, at the head of 15,000 men to capture the French Sugar Islands, his forces eventually sailing for St Lucia on April 26th 1796 (*Dictionary of National Biography*). He wanted to capture St Lucia because it was strategically placed with deep water anchorage at Castries Bay, which enabled larger ships to control the Caribbean. Rear Admiral Sir Hugh Christian KB led the fleet that effected a landing onto the island in Longueville Bay, where Major-General Campbell was ordered to disembark with 1700 men, where they were fired at from Pigeon Island. The troops that were landed were protected by the 74 gunner *Ganges*, whose captain was Robert MacDonall, and the 18 gunner *Pelican*, under Commander John Clarke Searle. Two more landings were made in reinforcing the island, one was on 27th April in Choc Bay, and disembarked near the village of Choc. They were initially attacked by a force of 500 defenders who then retired to Morne Chabot, which was in a commanding position. Morne Chabot had to be captured in order to attempt to take Morne Fortune, where 2000 Brigands – a force of slaves who were fighting for their freedom rather than through any inclination to support either the French or the British were in position (see *National Trust Guide, St Lucia* dated Feb-27th 1997). Two detachments from the British army, under the command of Brigadier-General Hope, were ordered to march that evening to attack it on two sides, which they did by marching along narrow trackways, from which they fought a series of attacks and counter attacks. Forty to fifty of the enemy were killed in this encounter, but in a further counter attack by the defenders on the grenadiers lead by Liet-Colonel MacDonald of 55th regiment several officers and 40 or 50 men were killed, so both sides had their share of casualties. A third landing in Anse La Raye on the 29th April, which was ordered by General Morshead, was the place where Captain Richard Lane successfully landed 800 men from his 32 gunner *Astria*, and from the *Bulldog*, whose commander was George Frederick Ryves.

This large group were co-operating in the campaign to capture this island – the fort of Morne Chabot was successfully taken on April 29th – and Chazeur later. On May 3rd an attack was carried out on some batteries, which resulted in heavy British casualties, and this was repeated on 17th May, in an assault on Vigie – both were repulsed. The French retreated to the fort of Morne Fortune where, after heavy bombardment from 24-pounder cannons and the remorseless onslaught of the the King's Shropshire Light infantry and the 24th regiment of Inniskillings – who attacked with bayonets fixed after being ordered to do so by General Moore, the defenders surrendered.

On May 24th the whole island capitulated. Two thousand men were allowed to march out of Fort Charlotte, where they had finally taken refuge, in the middle of a road lined both by the Inniskillings and Shropshire regiments. The bravery of the British forces is beyond question, yet the defenders were paid tribute because they had struggled courageously against overwhelming numbers of British troops, and their capitulation was a dignified affair.

On page 75 (Appendix to the Chronicle) of the *Annual Register* for 1796 are recorded the Articles for Capitulation. These are signed by Ralph Abercromby, Hugh C. Christian, Gottens, and Goyrand, at Morne Duchasseaux, St Lucia, May 25th, 1796. Article No 6 states:

6. The garrison shall pile their arms at the place appointed for that purpose and shall immediately be sent to France. The officers shall be allowed to take with them their wives and children.

Ans. The arms to be piled on the glacis without the fort. Answer has already been given as to the disposal of the garrison. The officers may dispose of their wives and children as they please.

By June, the islands of St Vincent and Grenada were captured, and the battle was over. The letter (see page 92) dated 4th October 1796 from Lord Grenville to the Lord Mayor of London showed effectively that those who died in the wreck of *The London* had only seventy four days days left to live.

§

The following letters to the Admiralty Office are extremely interesting:

Gentlemen,

I am commanded by their Lordships commissioners of the Admiralty to send you information, the inclosed copy of a letter which I have received from Liet. Gaydon, Regulating Officer at Ilfracombe, giving an account of the Loss of 'The London' of London, Transport with part of her crew, and to signify their Lordships' direction to you to give such directions respecting the people who may have been saved, as the circumstances of the case require.

Evan Nepean.'

(ADM/MT/416, Letters relating to prisoners of war 1796-1799).

The letter Mr Nepean was speaking of is the following:

'Admiralty Office, 12th October, 1796.

'Sir,

I beg you will inform their Lordships that last night at half after eight 'The London' transport of London, one of 'The Ganges' Convoy with French Prisoners, in coming for this harbour, a heavy squall took and forced her upon the rocks; the vessel went to pieces before day light; painful it is to me to inclose the return.'

The point is clarified here, absolutely, that *The London* was part of *The Ganges* convoy, even if it were as earlier described 'a straggler'. Lord Grenville's letter (see page 92) of 4th October 1796 showed that, at the time, he was convinced that all of *The Ganges* convoy had arrived safely. As shown, *The London* was some days behind and it was not until after Lord Grenville's letter had been written that the wreck occurred.

§

The letter to Richard Allard Governor of Stapleton prison, Bristol (quoted in full on page 87) which was unearthed by HTV and shown in their documentary clearly proves that there were survivors from the wreck of *The London*:

> .....*as they are chiefly, if not all naturals of the West Indies, we direct you to make what they suffer as little as possible from the coldness of the season.*

It is clear from the *Ilfracombe Customs Book* that upwards of 40 persons drowned in the wreck of *The London*, in the evening of 9th October 1796. The previous letters and documents clarify the point that *The London* was indeed carrying black West Indian and other prisoners, some of whom escaped drowning, and were carried in a smaller vessel to Stapleton Prison in Bristol, after 27th October 1796.

In the *Public Records Office*, there are the records of each survivor registered as sick or hurt. These records are known as those of the *Sick and Hurt Board* (in books ADM/103/41). These documents list the names of these survivors, one of whom was Col. Commandant, Heaurmaux, of Morne Fortune (Fort Charlotte) and his wife. They were ultimately paroled to Chippenham on December 8th 1796.

This was not to be the fate of the black survivors. In addition to their name (and number) there is information listing the name of the ship upon which they had been transported; their *Nationality*; the *Quality* of the prisoner; the *Date* received into custody; whether *Disposed* of; when *Disposed* of; and how *Disposed of*.

The ship is *The London*. The *Quality* of Col. Hermaux is listed as *Soldier* and his *Nationality* as *French*. Without fail the prisoners who are listed as only having Christian names (these make up the vast majority) are given as their *Nationality* either African or Carribean. Equally without fail their *Quality* is described as *Slave*.

§

139

A letter that was sent to me on 24th February 1997 by John Penny of *Fishponds Local History Society*, in Bristol. It concerned the wreck of *The London*, which he had read about in *The Times* on the same day. The letter, which is composed of two pages of history about the Admiralty Prison at Stapleton, and included an engraving by J.P. Malcolm that had been published in the *Gentleman's Magazine* (May 1814), was very useful and interesting. John wrote:

...With the outbreak of the Revolutionary War in 1793 the Admiralty Prison at Stapleton, one of the largest in the country, (now on the outskirts of Bristol and less than a mile from my house) was reopened to house some of the large numbers of military personnel which it was expected would be captured by British forces. It went on to house many thousands over the next 21 years, including a fairly large number of coloured French troops taken in the West Indies. As Negro men were on 'The London', a ship chartered by the Admiralty, they were almost certainly French troops rather than Slaves, which anyway would have been kept in the West Indies to help in the British possessions.

Clearly the word *slaves* had struck a nerve in Bristol. My evidence I believe clarifies the point – black prisoners were *treated as* slaves; in this instance the term means one and the same thing. They were brought to England and disposed of via Cartels, who would have traded them or exchanged them for soldiers or other prisoners-of-war. John's letter continues:

the fact that they were chained in the hold was not surprising, as this was normal practice at this time where prisoners were concerned.

There is no doubt that these prisoners *were* chained in the hold, and the fact that some of them died there is beyond dispute. John continues with interesting information regarding Stapleton Prison:

A single block of the old prison still survives as the nurses' home in what is today Blackberry Hill Hospital, and it was here in the 1950s that a number of prisoner burials were unearthed during the excavation for the new Somerdale Ward. These were bodies which had just been thrown into rough unmarked graves within the prison walls and remained unknown until the contractors arrived. I personally found several skulls and numerous bones which had been dumped along with other spoil in a nearby quarry, but the powers-that-be took little notice and did all they could to make sure that as few people as possible found out about it.

This was written to me just as I about to experience a similar scenario regarding the *powers-that-be*. As the early news reports began to appear it seemed that some people in Bristol were taking offence purely because prisoners bones had been found and given the label (by the media – not by me) *slaves*. It was suggested to me on more than one occasion that it was not possible that these people were being transported to Bristol as slaves. It baffled and disturbed me.

§

In 1997 the discovery of the article by Mrs Slade-King in the *Transactions of the Devonshire Association* (1879) seems to have done as much as anything to fuel the controversy. Her words, still seem somehow haunting:
This Rapparee Cove was the scene of a dismal wreck, nearly a century since, of a Bristol ship, with slaves on board. Their corpses were denied Christian burial, and their skulls are now at times turned up in neighbouring fields. Tradition says that many of them were drowned with iron fetters on their legs.

I have no evidence about skulls being found in neighbouring fields, but fetters have been found. From what I can discover of Mrs Slade-King there is no reason that she should describe the victims as slaves if she believed them to be prisoners-of-war. She was fully aware of the history of the Napoleonic wars and the tradition she speaks of seems to have been well founded. Such accounts passed from generation to generation are apparent in another source, a book called *Grandfathers' Stories*, which are cuttings from the *Ilfracombe Chronicle* of the 1870s. The following is a recital of a verbal traditions concerning the wreck of *The London*:

Tonight... brings before my mind as vividly as fifty years ago, the fearful wreck which took place in the channel, just before my poor old father was overtaken by a storm, and perished in sight of home... Well, it was about the time that George Sommers was plying his waggon between Ilfracombe and Barum; perhaps as long as 72 years ago, that this fearful wreck took place. It was late in the evening when a gun was heard faintly booming in the distance, and a fine vessel was seen in distress. Who fired the gun is a question I cannot answer, but it was thought most probably it was some of the crew, for the master of the vessel wanted no assistance as it turned out. Finding that he was in a position from which he could not extricate himself, it was supposed that he had determined to die rather than let it be known that he was trading with a human freight; that his vessel was laden with fellow beings as slaves. An Ilfracombe pilot bravely ventured out in response to the signal, but was not allowed to board her. 'Where are you from?' demanded the pilot. 'From hell – bound for damnation,' was the awful answer given by the ruffian captain, who had on board such invaluable treasure – a cargo of human life, with gold and spices, the worth of which none shall ever know, or as to how it came together none shall ever answer. 'Pilot, away!' exclaimed the captain, 'We want no assistance: we're bound to perish!' and, alas! soon the assertion was realised, and the noble vessel sank beneath the gurgling waters, amidst the agonizing cries and shrieks of those on board, thus ruthlessly and desperately deprived of precious life. In the morning the beach was covered with the bodies of the unfortunate Negroes, washed up on the tide; and amongst them – a strange and pitiful exception! – like a pearl amongst rubies – was a lovely creature, a youthful lady, A naked lily fair, lying dead and cold. Whether it was the body of a captive, or the captain's wife, none could ever tell, but the sea had made no distinction between the white and the black victims. As the waves moved

142

the sand on the beach, heaps of shining coins in gold met the sight of the astonished inhabitants, who were busily removing the dead bodies to the out-houses of the Britannia Hotel. The sight was a wondrous and not unwelcome one. Eagerly they rushed to the treasure. The cry is raised by some one, 'Stop! first bury the dead.' They hesitated, but the inward voice of conscience re-echoed the mandate, and they returned to their sad work, and the bodies were hastily buried in the hill-side, this being the most convenient spot near at hand, there to rest until the resurrection morn, Whether the gold was got afterwards I don't recollect; but I daresay a good deal was secured.

Since the people who buried the bodies were in a hurry to recover the gold coins that were lying scattered around in the shingle, I find this account very plausible indeed.

If we next consider the words written below Walters depiction of the wreck of *The London*, (see page 62) which was probably painted in the early 19th century:

The old slaver London from St Lucia in the West Indies,

This could mean that *The London* was an old boat, or a frequent slave-ship from St Lucia in the West Indies. Further wording throws us off the scent by appearing to suggest that she was, at the time of the wreck, with Admiral Rodney's fleet:

She had been attached to Admiral Rodney's fleet in the West Indies and was bringing home to Bristol valuables, and 150 black prisoners, 46 people were drowned, 6 of whom were Ilfracombe seamen who went to their rescue.

There is a real possibility that *The London* was once attached to Lord Rodney's fleet, but not at the time of the wreck. The time of Admiral Rodney was several years earlier. We know from the Port (Customs) book, that upwards of 40 people were said to have drowned in the wreck, which is close to the estimate given by Walters. However, recent evidence suggests that only 31 prisoners arrived in Bristol as survivors. This would mean that there were only around 70 prisoners actually on *The London* – this contradiction remains unresolved. The bodies of the six local seamen said to have drowned may

143

The Admiralty Prison at Stapleton

167

half-legendary tales which prevail of their daring and their doings. Scarcely a cave or a crook but has some marvellous tale clinging around it of dismal shipwrecks,* or of the smugglers who frequented their secure fastnesses,* or of the dread of ghosts and spirits, by local horrors, and a wholesome doings. To this source we may trace such stories as "The Haunted Room of Chambercombe," "The Jew Pedlar of the Crowkerne Cave," "The Fugitive Murderer of the Spirit of the Tors," "The Jew Pedlar of the Tors," and the well-known "The Cairn Top," "The Churchyard, and a numerous progeny of dark doings which are still remembered round firesides of North Devon yeomen.

It is well and amply written in the pages of innumerable guide books how the rugged Ilfracombe of to-day, How meteorologists the smooth and trim watering-place has been fractional differences by which it seems to have wrangled over the greatest number of marks in a competitive examination with other health resorts! How roads and rails have linked it distant parish church is becoming a necessity of all modern cities, our once sion, which the rest of the world, and how by that westward exten- and the wild Tors are on their land side studded with pathways villas, and their bold sea fronts are carved with modern easy of access to adventurous donkey-chairs!

* The name Rapsane Cove, at the entrance of the harbour, and the mock hunting of the Earl of Tyrone, yearly celebrated till within a few years, in the adjoining chapel of Commemartin, are to be traced up to the scene of the Rebellion of 1698. This Rapsano Cove was the scene of a dismal wreck, nearly a century after. ... were denied Christian burial, with slaves on board. Their skulls are even now at times turned up in the neighbouring fields. Tradition says that many of them were drowned with iron fetters on their legs.

166 THE OLDER TIMES

pointed." So-called church restorers have ruthlessly destroyed the characteristic features of the font; but evidence enough still remains to show its original form and date.

A portion of the present churchyard was the muscular howling-green and wrestling-ring, from whence the parochial Christians of those days used their hats, to escort their champions, adorned with silver spoons in their hats, as early as 1315 in the new demolished gallery. Ilfracombe, and called forth ecclesiastical Fairs held "in Cemeterio de Ilfracombe," and the diocese. They most produced tumult and bloodshed, on the public green, and censure from the then Bishop, at first on the consecrated ground of probably were commenced on to the extended churchyard.

Oliver, in his Ecclesiastical Antiquities, vol. ii., p. 135, gives also information as to the history of the incumbents, commencing with Henry de Monte Forti, who was admitted on Friday in Whitsun week, on the presentation of the Henry de Campo Arnulphi, to furnishes a list of the present, thirty-nine vicars have succeeded whom the charter of their sacred office, a space of time covered by that date to each other in the reigns of twenty-five English monarchs. From him and the other sources we find there were four oratories in the parish; but only one remaining is, "Sancti Nicholi supra Portum Maris," used as a lighthouse as far back as 1522.

The interior timber, and the niche on which was placed the statue of the saint of sailors, remain in situ. The building, has been turned into a dwelling-house; but much of the oak external character of the building, was opened modern roof has prevented its decay. The south walls. A rock-hewn grave was opened but has not contributed many names to the Worthies therein a few years since under the Romish Church.

Ilfracombe has known as of Devon; but John Cutcliffe, a writer of credit, Damago Farm in Johannes de Rupecissa, who was born at Avignon for his the fourteenth century, and died in prison at Sir W. Herle, attempts to reform the Romish Church; and a contemporary of deserve mention. Justice of Common Pleas, who was Chambercombe, his, and lived at Chambernon Wick, now Chambercombe.

Chief temptations and facilities which Ilfracombe afforded for evading the Excise duties rendered the smuggler's a favourite and lucrative calling. It is not the purpose of notes like these to chronicle the

never have been found, and this may account for the fact that they are not mentioned in the Parish Church register of burials.

Another letter written by Evan Nepean from the Admiralty Office, 27th October 1796 – just eighteen days after the wreck, states:

Gentn.,

I am commanded by my Lords Commissioners of the Admiralty to signify their direction to you to let me know the number of Prisoners of War, lately arrived from the West Indies, distinguishing the Blacks; their Lordships being desirous of knowing the proportions which men in health bear to the number sick, on which a report has been [sent] *from the Comsrs. For sick & Wounded.*

I am Gentn.,
Your most humble servant
Evan Nepean.
Commissioners for Transport.

We are not told why the black prisoners needed to be distinguished from the others. Common sense suggests it has to be because they were considered slaves and the entries of the *Sick and Hurt Board* supports this reasoning.

These entries are of enormous interest. It is with this list of prisoners that we have arrived at the answer — amongst those listed from numbers 2681-2711 are 4 *Soldiers* from France; 11 *Mulatto Slaves* from the West Indies; and 14 *Negro Slaves* from Africa. This is plain for all to see, because at the top of the first column on the second page, is the clear heading *Prisoners Names*, which is a list of all the prisoners names who were received into custody in Bristol from 1793-1800. At the head of the next column is their *Quality*. All the West Indians without exception are listed as Mulatto slaves; all the Negroes are listed as African slaves and all soldiers as French. All of these sick prisoners came from *The London*. Some were discharged dead in hospital between 22nd December 1796 and 15th February 1797, and others, arguably the more fortunate ones are listed as being disposed of via the *Nancy* or *Smallbridge* Cartels.

Appendix A

High Tides, Storms & Aftermath

There were various plus tides in Rapparee Cove in September and October 1997, and the tide on 18th of September promised to be much higher than the 10.4m forecast, due to it being the highest tide for many years. However, it was a calm day and the sea was like a millpond, so I did not visit the site on this occasion. Two days later I looked at the site, and it was clear that the sea had washed most of the reinstated spoil from the July excavation away and the stones and boulders were washed clean. Also the raised pile of stones, erected by the members of the *African Reparation Movement* members had been washed clean away, with no trace remaining. None of these high tides damaged the sloping bank to any degree, just a slight slippage on one occasion occurred.

The council, I believe, are eventually going to repair the site, when and if, some money becomes available. An article in the *North Devon Journal* dated 27th November 1997, chiefly concerning the new theatre in Ilfracombe, also reported that money may be available later for any scheme for the Rapparee bones.

The start of January 1998 was particularly stormy with gale force winds blowing from the 1st day of the new year. The 4th was a Sunday and at 9am a gale was still blowing, so I decided to look at the tide times to see if it was worth a visit to Rapparee Cove. Fortunately the tide was high by 9.45am, so I had time to grab my camera and some waterproof clothing, before driving over.

I decided to walk around to the cove, via the muddy lower Hillsborough footpath and was halfway down the steps that descend from above the stage when I paused, hoping for some decent high vantage point shots. There was no beach area uncovered by this time, and the tide was only 8.8m but the wind action on the sea was bringing in huge breakers that smashed on the rocks all around amidst the cauldron of white surf and spray that thundered into the stormy cove. I was watching, waiting for a suitable action shot, when I was taken by surprise as a huge wave thundered over the stone building at the bottom of the steps and hit the cliff behind. The salt water crashed onto the twisting path and ran down behind the shelter before dividing itself into small streams. Beside the path, waves were surging into the site, dragging rock and soil back out into a trough that now exposed the sloping ramp and wooden post which an instant before had been completely submerged. Huge waves smashed against the rock face to the right of the site and the spray was flung half way up the cliff by force of the raging gale. The building on the far side of the cove was mercilessly battered by the ferocity of the storm and constantly dwarfed by the height of the waves.

The whole scene was a violent white cauldron of destructive force, its energy released onto the site and rocks all around. I could visualise the instant destruction of any ship trapped in this hell's mouth, with no escape. If the conditions on the evening of Sunday 9th October 1796 were similar to this then it was a death trap, make no mistake.

The 9th October 1997 commemorated the wreck of *The London*. It was raining very hard that evening, and my wife Roz, councillor Doug Ray and I visited the cove on that dark wet evening, just after 8pm. With our torches shining into the wet gloomy night and the steady rain slightly driving into our faces, we walked carefully towards the dark cove and down the slippery steps towards the site, which was hidden from view in the far corner of the dreary cove. It had been two hundred and one years since the wreck of *The London* took place at 8.30pm. On arriving at the foot of the steps below *the balcony* we made our way carefully across the wet sand to the site. I then drove in a one metre high, home-made wooden cross, with the words that the Reverend Jackson-Stevens had written for me earlier that day, at his Ilfracombe vicarage. The words were wrapped in clear plastic to protect them from the rain, and pinned to the cross of larch wood. We laid flowers, some picked from our garden and some donated by Doug's daughter, before standing with our backs to the roar of the sea and reciting in prayer the words that were now pinned to the cross:

> *May their souls by the mercy of God now rest in peace.*
> *Our Father who art in Heaven,*
> *Hallowed be thy name.*
> *Thy Kingdom come, thy will be done*
> *On Earth as it is in Heaven*
>
> *Amen*

We then made our way back across the cove through the torch-lit rain, and up the slippery steps to our car.

§

Roz and I returned the following morning to take some more photographs with the benefit of daylight. It was a grey day, drizzling and as we were leaving the cove an elderly man dressed in thick overcoat, scarf and cloth cap passed us as he descended the steps of the main footpath, walking his dog. We exchanged a 'good morning' and the man continued across the cove halting as he reached the grave site. Bowing his head removed his cloth cap and stood with his hands clasped in silent remembrance before continuing on his way and leaving the cove by the Hillsborough steps.

I visited the cove a week or so later, and only the post of the cross I had hammered into the site remained. Doug's flowers were dry and had been moved to the right hand side outside the standing section of wall. The flowers Roz had laid were completely missing – probably due to the tide.

§

On 5th February 1998 I met police sergeant Angus Cottey in Ilfracombe Museum. Sergeant Cottey was conducting some research as part of a degree course in Forensic Archaeology and had just consulted the file on *The London* which is lodged at the museum. During the course of our conversation he told me that he had been present at Ilfracombe police station when Paul Howard had taken in a bag of bones from Rapparee Cove about three years before. The sergeant was aware of my efforts

149

to trace these bones and advised me to telephone the morgue at the North Devon District Hospital and ask for somebody called Bill.

However, though I had telephoned several times, it was some weeks before I managed to contact Bill, prompted to further effort by a conversation Roz had with Paul Howard when they met by coincidence in the *Sea Swallow* Chinese take-away. Paul re-affirmed that he *had* found a skull at Rapparee, and it was this which inspired me to try again at the morgue in Barnstaple.

I rang there about 2pm on 8th April 1998, and was put through to Bill. He enquired as to my reasons for wanting to locate the skull concerned, and I told him of my meeting sergeant Cottey, and that I was writing the story of the events surrounding the wreck of *The London*. He then told me that there were no records kept of any bones handed in to the morgue three years before. Dismayed, I asked him what happens to any bones that can't be identified, and he said, "We keep them," and "we put them into a box."

There were several boxes, and Bill kindly offered to help in any way if I cared to come in and look through them. At last, hope and faith restored I stammered, "Can I come in... now?"

To which Bill answered, "If you like."

I rushed outside, jumped into my car and headed for Barnstaple. As I entered the hospital grounds I followed the road around towards the tall chimney of the boiler house and parked at the back of the building where I knew the morgue was located. Outside a pair of double doors is located a large bell, rang only occasionally by funeral directors. A minute passed before the door was opened and I was welcomed inside. After I was interviewed (for security reasons) I explained further why I was there. I was then led into a side office by a mortician whom I faintly recognised and found myself in a small room where the boxes of ancient, unidentified bones were kept on a top shelf. I assisted the official who had seemed to conjure a pair of steps from out of nowhere, by taking three boxes and a large paper bag, and placing them on an empty mortuary table.

Labels in two of the boxes and the bag eliminated these from my search, but I instantly recognised the weathering on a fragmented skull in the third box. This type of wear had been present on other bones from Rapparee Cove – it was distinguishable from the bones in the other boxes, which were unweathered. Also distinguishable, were the white teeth that Paul Howard had told me of, and they were all there to see, some being still in their jaw sockets, the rest strewn inside the box with the rest of the fragmented skull. It was also clear that the teeth needed several fillings, which may indicate a high sugar diet. The two broken jaw-bones fitted together perfectly, to form an almost pointed lower jaw. There were three molars on the left side, and three molars and a pre-molar on the right side of the lower jaw, still in place. The upper two halves holding the top teeth fitted together perfectly, more in a semicircular fashion. On the left side there were two molars, and on the right side three molars and one pre-molar.

There were thirty one teeth in all, one of which was rotted off; an abscess at its root.

Appendix B

The Convoy in Choc Bay

On the 3rd of May 1998, I came across copies of two documents, which to my surprise had been overlooked at an earlier date. These documents are difficult to follow as the writing is feint and hard to read. I decided to trace the words in pen in order to clarify their meaning.

The first document (ADM 1/2131) was written by Evan Nepean, on behalf of Captain Rob. MacDonall of *The Ganges*, the ship which led the convoy of 103 ships. At the time of the letter (9th December 1796) she was berthed at Portsmouth.

MacDonall dictated his letter to Nepean with regard to an order he had been given to take on board *The Ganges* from *The Jupio* Major General Hunter; and Brigadiers Keppel, Howe and White. He had then landed General Hunter at Martinique, but he complains that he was never paid his allowance.

Then he begs the Lord Commissioners of the Admiralty, that by the order of Sir John Laforcy he had carried:

General —— and many more officers from Martinico to St Vincent. Also the Generals Campbel, Graham, Hope, Moore and all their staff and field officers that had made the landing on St Lucia, under the protection of the Ganges from Barbatoes to Martinico, and from Martinico to their landing, and after the island was taken was left with the Naval Command there to settle that island, and on my arrival to St Kitts, I was obliged to take on board the Ganges the famous black General Marinier, who often defeated the English Generals at St Lucia and St Vincent and made the capitulation with Sir Ralf Abercromby that their Lordships may be pleased to order such reimbursements for the unavoidable expenses I have been at for the accommodation of the service I am with great regard.

Rob. McDonnall.

The other document (ADM 1/2133), dated 15th January 1797, gives an insight into events while the transports were still in Choc Bay awaiting the order to sail. In this, another letter written by Evan Nepean on behalf of Robert MacDonall, he writes:

> A writ having been served on me issuing from the court of the Common Pleas and responsible on the 20th instant at the suit of Jeremiah Williams. I must take the liberty of stating for their Lordships information, the cause of the action, and trust that as the transaction took place in the necessary course of my duty, they will be pleased to direct their solution to conduct my defence, at the publics expense.

Captain MacDonall, it seems, had been left commanding the island of St Lucia after its surrender in June, and had been in charge of the three thousand prisoners, in a number of transports, as well as his majesty's ships. Jeremiah Williams was a seaman aboard one of these transports, which was used to board the prisoners whilst awaiting orders to sail, and every night a great number of the mutinous prisoners had been escaping to the shore – where they promptly joined up with other armed black *Brigands*. In this way they posed a very great threat to the lives of all the opposing forces.

It subsequently came to light that a conspiracy was afoot. MacDonall suggests that there was a plan in which a woman intended to cut the mooring ropes holding the transport to which Williams belonged. This transport would then drift to shore, and once there the black prisoners – said to be of 'desperate caste' would escape and form an offensive to 'retake' the island. It was a woman who had been carrying messages from ship to ship, and Williams was seen rowing a woman out to board his ship, in full view of *The Ganges*. They were spotted, and Captain MacDonall issued orders that 'no women' should be allowed aboard any of the transports, and any already on board 'should be immediately sent ashore.' Williams had been caught red handed disobeying an order, and was given six lashes aboard *The Ganges*.

After the flotilla had eventually sailed, the Captain and 1st mate on William's transport died, and Williams brought her home as master, which was mentioned to their Lordships, in Williams favour.

There may have been a plot, or conspiracy as MacDonall had suggested, and the motive behind it was that the prisoners knew in their hearts that they were destined to end up once more as slaves. They had capitulated honourably, and were allowed to march out in an honourable way – yet it seemed that they were about to embark upon a journey to where they would never taste freedom again.

The British Chief Justice Lord Mansfield, in an important case in 1772, involving *'whether a master who brought a slave to England in attendance upon him could legally require him to return to slavery in the West Indies, or whether a slave was free as soon as he reached English soil,'* decided in favour of the slave. However, in reality the situation was much more confused. In the Annual Register for 1796, the Articles of Capitulation (Page 80), records that:

2. *The negroes &c. are to return to their respective proprietors*

In Parry and Sherlock (1985, page 166) it states that in 1794, whilst under attack by the British, Negro troops in Saint Dominique under the command of Toussaint l'Ouverture were alarmed by the English progress, and feared the restoration of slavery which an English victory would entail. Thus, even if eventually the prisoners in the transports were returned to their island of origin, via the cartels, they would still be returning to slavery if the English forces won. What is worse, is the fact that the cartels were not only formed to exchange prisoners, but were paid for their services (Murrey,1893, page 139).

According to Williams, E. in *Columbus to Castro* (1970, p.250), the French had 'decreed the total abolition of slavery in the French dominions, in 1794', yet according to *Chambers Miscellany* of c1865 this was more a freedom of convenience (See Appendix C).

It would seem logical to me that whether the Islands were in French or British control, every black or mulatto prisoner aboard the transports would know they were destined to be returned to a life of slavery. Williams (p.250) states:

every Negro and Mulatto knew what that meant, slavery for the former, political and social inferiority for the latter.'

Appendix C

Toussaint l'Ouverture

During my research I came across, in Volume 10 of *Chambers Miscellany* (c1865) a short history entitled *Toussaint l'Ouverture and the Republic of Hayti*. This so effectively sums up the complex nature of the situation in the West Indies in the late 1700s that I have decided to broadly quote it here:

Hispaniola, St Domingo, or Hayti is not only one of the largest, but also one of the most beautiful and productive islands in the West Indies, extending a length of 390 miles by a breadth of from 60 to 150. Formerly a Spanish colony, by the mid 1700s it had come largely under the control of the French, with the smaller, eastern part of the island still considered as belonging to Spain.

From 1776 to 1789, the French colony was at the height of its prosperity. To use the words of a French historian, everything had received a prodigious improvement. Roads had been opened across the asperities of the mountains; safe pathways had been constructed over chasms; bridges had been built over rivers which had formerly been passed with danger by means of ox-skin boats; the winds, the tides, the currents had been studied, so as to secure to ship's safe-sailing and convenient harbourage. Villas of pretty but simple architecture had risen along the borders of the sea, while mansions of greater magnificence embellished the interior. Public buildings, hospitals, aqueducts, fountains, and baths rendered life agreeable and healthy; all the comforts of the Old World had been transported to the New. In 1789 the population of the colony was 665,000; and of its staple products, it exported in that year 68,000,000 pounds of coffee and 163,000,000 pounds of sugar. The French had some reason to be proud of St Domingo; it was their best colony, and it promised, as they thought, to remain for ages in their possession. Many French families of note had emigrated to the island, and settled in it as planters; and both by means of commerce, and the passing to and fro of families, a constant intercourse was maintained between the colony and the mother-country.

Circumstances eventually proved that the expectation of keeping permanent possession of St Domingo was likely to be fallacious. The constitution of society in the island was unsound. In this, as in all the European colonies in the new World, negro slavery prevailed. To supply the demand for labour, an importation of slaves from Africa had been going on for some time at the rate of about 20,000 a year; and thus at the time at which we are now arrived there was a population of between 500,000 and 600,000. These negroes constituted an overwhelming majority of the inhabitants of the colony, for the whites did not amount to more than 40,000. But besides the whites and the negroes, there was a third class in the population, arising from the intermixture of the white and negro races. These were *people of colour*, including persons of all varieties of hue, from the perfect stable of the freed negro, to the most delicate tinge marking remote negro ancestry in a white man. Of these various classes of mulattoes, at the time of which we are now speaking, there were about 30,000 in the colony.

Although perhaps less cruelly treated than others in a state of hopeless servitude, the negroes of St Domingo were not exempt from the miseries which usually accompany slavery; yet they were not so ignorant as not to know their rights as members of the human family. In the year 1685, Louis XIV had published a *code noir*, or black code, containing a number of regulations for the humane treatment of the negroes in the colonies. Still, there were miseries inseparable from the system, and which could not be mitigated; and in St Domingo, as in all the other colonies of the New World, slavery was maintained by the cruelties of the whip and the branding-iron.

The condition of the mulatto population deserves particular attention. Although nominally free, and belonging to no individual master, these mulattoes occupied a very degraded social position. Regarded as public property, they were obliged to serve in the colonial militia without any pay. They could hold no public trust or employment, nor fill any of the liberal professions – law, medicine, divinity, &c. They were not allowed to sit at table with a white, to occupy the same place at church, to bear the same name, or to be buried in the same spot. Offences which in a white man were visited with scarcely any punishment, were punished with great severity when committed by a mulatto. There was one circumstance, however, in the condition of the mulattoes, which operated as a balance to all those indignities, and enabled them to become formidable in the colony – they were allowed to acquire and to hold property in any amount. Able, energetic, and rendered doubly intent upon the acquisition of wealth by the power which it gave them, many of these mulattoes or people of colour became rich, purchased estates, and equalled the whites as planters. Not only so, but, possessing the tastes of

156

Europeans and gentlemen, they used to quit St Domingo and pay occasional visits to what they as well as the whites regarded as their mother-country. It was customary for wealthy mulattoes to send their children to Paris for their education. It ought to be remarked also respecting the mulatto part of the population of St Domingo, that they kept aloof from both the pure whites and the pure negroes. Such was the state of society in the colony of St Domingo in the year 1789-90, when the French Revolution broke out.

§

Although situated at a distance of 3500 miles from France, St Domingo was not long in responding to the political agitations which broke out in Paris in 1789. When the news reached the colony that the king had summoned the States-general, all the island was in a ferment. Considering themselves entitled to share in the national commotion, the colonists held meetings, passed resolutions, and elected eighteen deputies to be sent home to sit in the States-general as representatives. The eighteen deputies reached Versailles a considerable time after the States-general had commenced their sittings and constituted themselves the National Assembly; and their arrival not a little surprised that body, who probably never expected deputies from St Domingo, or who at all events thought eighteen deputies too many for one colony. Accordingly, it was with some difficulty that six of them were allowed to take their seats. At that time colonial gentlemen were not held in great favour at Paris. Among the many feelings which then simultaneously stirred and agitated that great metropolis, there had sprung up a strong feeling against negro slavery. Whether the enthusiasm was kindled by the recent proceedings of Clarkson and Wilberforce in London, or whether it was derived by the French themselves from the political maxims then afloat, the writers and speakers of the Revolution made the iniquity of negro slavery one of their most frequent and favourite topics; and there had just been founded in Paris a society called *Amis des Noirs*, or Friends of the Blacks, of which the leading revolutionists were members. These *Amis des Noirs* seem partly to have been influenced by a real benevolent zeal on behalf of the negroes, and partly to have employed the movement for the emancipation of the slaves in the colonies merely as an instrument to assist them in their home-politics. To them negro slavery was a splendid instance of despotism. They succeeded in raising a prejudice against the colonists and their interests. When a planter from the sugar islands made his appearance in the streets of Paris, he was looked at as a walking specimen of a despot who had grown rich at the expense of the blood and the agonies of the fellow-men. The mulattoes, on the other hand, then resident in Paris, the young men who had been sent over for their education, as well as those who chanced to have come on a visit, were diligently sought out by the *Amis des Noirs*, and became public pets. Amiable, well educated, and interesting in their appearance, it gave great point and effect to the eloquence of a revolutionist orator to have one of these young mulattoes by his side when he was speaking; and when, at the conclusion of a passage in praise of liberty, the orator would turn and indicate with his finger his coloured friend, or when, yielding to French impulse, he would throw his arms round him and embrace him with sobs, how could the meeting be unmoved or the cheering fail to be loud and long?

The intelligence of what was occurring at Paris gave great alarm in St Domingo. When the celebrated declaration of rights, asserting all men to be 'free and equal,' reached the island along with the news of the proceedings of the *Amis des Noirs*, the whites, almost all of whom were interested in the preservation of slavery, looked upon their ruin as predetermined. They had no objection to freedom in the abstract – freedom which should apply only to themselves – but they considered it a violation of all decency to speak of black men, mere *property*, having political rights. What disheartened the whites gave encouragement to the mulattoes. Rejoicing in the idea that the French people were their friends, they became turbulent, and rose in arms in several places, but were without much difficulty put down. Two or three whites, who were enthusiastic revolutionists, sided with the insurgents; and one of them, M. de Beaudierre, fell a victim to the fury of the colonists. The negro population of the island remained quiet; the contagion of revolutionary sentiments had not yet reached them.

When the National Assembly heard of the alarm which the new constitution had excited in the colonies, they saw the necessity for adopting some measures to allay the storm; and accordingly, on the 8th of March 1790, they passed a resolution disclaiming all intention to legislate sweepingly for the internal affairs of the colonies, and authorising each colony to mature a plan for itself in its own legislative assembly (the Revolution having superseded the old system of colonial government by royal officials, and given to each colony a legislative assembly, consisting of representatives elected by the colonists), and submit the same to the National Assembly. This resolution, which gave great dissatisfaction to the *Amis des Noirs* in Paris, produced a temporary calm in St Domingo. For some time nothing was to be heard but the bustle of elections throughout the colony; and at length, on the 16th of April 1790, the general assembly met, consisting of 213 representatives. With great solemnity, and at the same time with great enthusiasm, they began their work – a work which was to be nothing less than a complete reformation of all that was wrong in St Domingo, and the preparation of a new constitution for the future government of the island. The colonists were scarcely less excited about this miniature revolution of their own, than the French nation had been about the great revolution of the mother-country. All eyes were upon the proceedings of the assembly; and at length, on the 28th May, it published the results of its deliberations in the form of a new constitution, consisting of ten articles. The provisions of this new constitution, and the language in which they were expressed, were astounding: they amounted, in fact, to the throwing off of all allegiance to the mother-country. This very unforeseen result created great commotion in the island. The cry rose everywhere that the assembly was rebelling against the mother-country; some districts recalled their deputies, declaring they would have no concern with such presumptuous proceedings. The governor-general, M. Peynier, was bent on dissolving the assembly altogether; riots were breaking out in various parts of the island, and a civil war seemed impending, when in one of its sittings the assembly, utterly bewildered and terrified, adopted the extraordinary resolution of going on board a ship-of-war then in the harbour, and sailing bodily to France to consult with the National Assembly. Accordingly, on the 8th of August, eighty-five members, embarked on board the *Leopard*, and the vessel set sail for Europe.

In the meantime, the news of the proceedings of the colonial assembly had reached France, and all parties, royalists as well as revolutionists, were indignant at what they called the impudence of these colonial legislators. The *Amis des Noirs* of course took an extreme interest in what was going on; and under their auspices, an attempt was made to take advantage of the disturbances prevailing in the island for the purpose of meliorating the condition of the coloured population. A young mulatto named James Ogé was then residing in Paris, whither he had been sent by his mother, a woman of colour, the proprietrix of a plantation in St Domingo. Ogé had formed the acquaintance of the Abbé Gregoire, Brissot, Robespierre, Lafayette, and other leading revolutionists connected with the society of the *Amis des Noirs*, and fired by the ideas which he derived from them, as well as directly instigated by their advice, he resolved to return to St Domingo, and, rousing the spirit of insurrection, become the deliverer of his enslaved race. Accordingly, paying a visit to America first, he landed in his native island on the 12th of October 1790, and announced himself as the redresser of all wrongs. Matters, however, were not yet ripe for an insurrection; and after committing some outrages with a force of 200 mulattoes, which was all he was able to raise, Ogé was defeated, and obliged, with one or two associates, to take refuge in the Spanish part of the island. M. Blanchelande succeeding M. Peynier as governor-general of the colony, demanded Ogé from the Spaniards; and in March 1791 the wretched young man, after betraying the existence of a wide-laid conspiracy among the mulattoes and negroes of the island, was broken alive upon the wheel.

All this occurred while the eighty-five members of the assembly were absent in France. They had reached that country in September 1790, and been well-received at first, owing to the novelty and picturesqueness of their conduct; but when they appeared before the National Assembly, that body treated them with marked insult and contempt. On the 11th of October, Barnave proposed and carried a decree annulling all the acts of the colonial assembly, dissolving it, declaring its members ineligible again for the same office, and detaining the eighty-five unfortunate gentlemen prisoners in France. Barnave, however, was averse to any attempt on the part of the National Assembly to force a constitution upon the colony against its will; and especially he was averse to any direct interference between the whites and the people of colour. These matters of internal regulation, he said, should be left to the colonists themselves; all that the National assembly should require of the colonists was, that they should act in the general spirit of the Revolution. Others, however, among whom were Gregoire, Brissot, Robespierre, and Lafayette, were for the home government dictating the leading articles of a new constitution for the colony; and especially they were for some assertion by the National Assembly of the equal citizenship of the coloured inhabitants of the colony. For some time the debate was carried on between these two parties; but the latter gradually gained strength, and the storm of public indignation which was excited by the news of the cruel death of Ogé gave them the complete victory.

Hurried on by a tide of enthusiasm, the National Assembly, on the 15th of May, passed a decree declaring all the people of colour in the French colonies, born of free parents, entitled to vote for members of the colonial judicatures, as well as to be elected to seats themselves. This decree of admission to citizenship concerned, it will be observed, the mulattoes and free blacks only; it did not affect the condition of the slave population.

In little more than a month this decree, along with the intelligence of all that had been said and done when it was passed, reached St Domingo.

The colony was thrown into convulsions. The white colonists stormed and raged, and there was no extremity to which, in the first outburst of their anger, they were not ready to go. The national cockade was trampled under foot. It was proposed to forswear allegiance to the mother-country, seize the French ships in the harbours, and the goods of French merchants, and hoist the British flag instead of the French. The governor-general, M Blanchelande, trembled for the results. But at length the fury of the colonists somewhat subsided: a new colonial assembly was convened: hopes began to be entertained that something might be effected by its labours, when lo! the news ran through the island like the tremor of an earthquake: 'The blacks have risen!' The appaling news was too true. The conspiracy, the existence of which had been divulged by Ogé before his execution, had burst into explosion. The outbreak had been fixed for the 25th of August; but the negroes, impatient as the time drew near, had commenced it on the night of the 22nd. The insurrection broke out first on a plantation near the town of Cape François; but it extended itself immediately far and wide; and the negroes rising on every plantation, first murdered their masters and their families and set fire to their houses, and then poured in to swell the insurgent army. The greater part of the mulattoes joined them, and took a leading share in the insurrection.

The insurrection was successful. Although the numerical loss of the insurgents had been greater than that of the whites, yet the latter saw that it was in vain to hold out longer against such a large body of foes. Accordingly, on the 11th of September, a truce was concluded between the whites and the mulattoes in the western province; and following this good example, the general assembly of the colony came to a resolution to admit the obnoxious decree of the 15th of May, which recognised the equal citizenship of all persons of colour born of free parents. As the refusal to admit this decree had been the pretext for the insurrection, this concession, along with some others, had the effect of restoring order; although, as may be readily conceived, the blacks, who gained nothing by the concession, were far from being conciliated or satisfied. The mulattoes however, were now gained over to the side of the whites, and the two together hoped to be able to keep the negroes in greater awe.

Meanwhile strange proceedings relative to the colonies were occurring in the mother-country. The news of the insurrection of the blacks had not had time to reach Paris; but the intelligence of the manner in which the decree of the 15th of May had been received by the whites in St Domingo had created great alarm. 'We are afraid we have been too hasty with that decree of ours about the rights of the mulattoes: it is likely, by all accounts, to occasion a civil war between them and the whites; and if so, we run the risk of losing the colony altogether.' This was the common talk of the politicians in Paris. Accordingly, they hastened to undo what they had done for four months before, and on the 24th of September the National Assembly actually repealed the decree of the 15th of May by a large majority. Thus the mother-country and the colony were at cross-purposes; for at the very moment that the colony was admitting the decree, the mother-country was repealing it.

The flames of war were immediately rekindled in the colony. 'The decree is repealed,' said the whites; 'we need not have been in such a hurry in making concessions to the mulattoes.' 'The decree is repealed,' said the mulattoes; 'the people in Paris are playing false with us; we must depend on ourselves in future. There is no possibility of coming to terms with the whites; either they must exterminate us, or we must exterminate them.' Such was the effect of the wavering conduct of the home government. All the horrors of August were re-enacted, and the year 1791 was concluded amid scenes of war, pestilence and bloodshed. The whites, collected in forts, and cities, bade defiance to the insurgents. The mulattoes and blacks fought on the same side, sometimes under one standard, sometimes in separate bands. A large colony of blacks, consisting of slaves broken loose from the plantations they had lived upon, settled in the mountains under two leaders named Jean François and Biassou, planted provisions for their subsistence, and watching for opportunities, made irruptions into the plains.

§

In daily jeopardy of their lives, and seeing no prospect of a return of prosperity, immense numbers of the white colonists were quitting the island. Many families had emigrated to the neighbouring island of Jamaica, many to the United States, and some even had sought refuge, like the royalists of the mother-country, in Great Britain. Through these persons, as well as through the refugees from the mother-country, overtures had been made to the British government, for the purpose of inducing it to take possession of the island of St Domingo, and convert it into a British colony; and in 1793, the British government, against which the French republic had now declared war, began to listen favourably to these proposals. General Williamson, the lieutenant-governor of Jamaica, was instructed to send troops from that island to St Domingo, and attempt to wrest it out of the hands of the French. Accordingly, on the 20th of September 1793, about 870 British soldiers, under Colonel

Whitelocke, landed in St Domingo – a force miserably defective for such an enterprise. The number of troops was afterwards increased, and the British were able to effect the capture of Port-au-Prince, and also some ships which were in the harbour. Alarmed by this success, the French Commissioners, Santhonax and Polverel, issued a decree abolishing negro slavery, at the same time inviting the blacks to join them against the British invaders. Several thousands did so; but the great majority fled to the hills, swelling the army of the negro chiefs, François and Biassou, and luxuriating in the liberty which they had so suddenly acquired.

It was at this moment of utter confusion and disorganisation, when British, French, Mulattoes and Blacks were all acting their respective parts in the turmoil, and all inextricably intermingled in a bewildering war, which was neither a foreign war, nor a civil war, nor a war of races, but a composition of all three – it was at this moment that Toussaint l'Ouverture appeared, the spirit and the ruler of the storm.

§

Toussaint l'Ouverture, one of the most extraordinary men of a period when extraordinary men were numerous, and beyond all question the highest specimen of negro genius the world has yet seen, was born in St Domingo, on the plantation of the Count de Noé, a few miles distant from Cape François, in the year 1743. His father and mother were African slaves on the count's estate. His father, it is said, was the second son of Gaou-Guinou, king of a powerful African tribe; but being taken prisoner by a hostile people, he was, according to the custom of the African nations, sold as a slave to some white merchants, who carried him to St Domingo, where he was purchased by the Count de Noé. Kindly treated by his master, the king's son scarcely regretted that he had been made a slave. He married a fellow-slave, a girl of his own country, and by her he had eight children, five sons and three daughters. Of the sons, Toussaint was the eldest. The negro boy grew up on the plantation on which his father and mother were slaves, performing such little services as he could; and altogether his life was as cheerful, and his work as easy, as that of any slave-boy in St Domingo. On Count Noé's plantation there was a black of the name of Pierre-Baptiste, a shrewd, intelligent man, who had acquired much information, besides having been taught the elements of what would be termed a plain European education by some benevolent missionaries. Between Pierre and young Toussaint an intimacy sprung up, and all that Pierre had learnt from the

163

missionaries, Toussaint learned from him. His acquisitions, says our French authority, amounted to reading, writing, arithmetic, a little Latin, and an idea of geometry. It was a fortunate circumstance that the greatest natural genius among the negroes of St Domingo was thus singled out to receive the unusual gift of a little instruction. Toussaint's qualifications gained him promotion; he was made the coachman of M. Bayou, the overseer of the Count de Noé – a situation as high as a negro could hope to fill. In this, and in still higher situations to which he was subsequently advanced, his conduct was irreproachable, so that while he gained the confidence of his master, every negro in the plantation held him in respect. Three particulars are authentically known respecting his character at this period of his life, and it is somewhat remarkable that all are points more peculiarly of moral than of intellectual superiority. He was noted, it is said, for an exceedingly patient temper, for great affection for brute animals, and for a strong unswerving attachment to one female whom he had chosen for his wife. It is also said that he manifested singular strength of religious sentiment. In person he was above the middle size, with a striking countenance, and a robust constitution, capable of enduring any amount of fatigue, and requiring little sleep.

Toussaint was about forty-eight years of age when the insurrection of the blacks took place in August 1791. Great exertions were made by the insurgents to induce a negro of his respectability and reputation to join them in their first outbreak, but he steadily refused. It is also known that it was owing to Toussaint's care and ingenuity that his master, M. Bayou, and his family escaped being massacred. He hid them in the woods for several days, visited them at the risk of his own life, secured the means of their escape from the island, and after they were settled in the United States, sent them such remittances as he could manage to snatch from the wreck of their property. Such conduct, in the midst of such barbarities as were then enacting, indicates great originality and moral independence of character. After his master's escape Toussaint, who had no tie to retain him longer in servitude, and who, besides, saw reason and justice in the struggle which his race was making for liberty, attached himself to the bands of negroes then occupying the hills, commanded by François and Biassou. In the negro army Toussaint at once assumed a leading rank; and a certain amount of medical knowledge, which he had picked up in the course of his reading, enabled him to unite the functions of army physician with those of military officer. Such was Toussaint's position in the end of the year 1793, when the British landed in the island.

§

It is necessary here to describe, as exactly as confusion will permit, the true state of parties in the island. The British, as we already know, were attempting to take the colony out of the hands of the French republic. and annex it to the crown of Great Britain; and in this design they were favoured by the few French royalists still resident in the island. The French commissioners, Santhonax and Polverel, on the other hand, men of the republican school, were attempting, with a motley army of French, mulattoes, and blacks, to beat back the British. The greater part of the mulattoes of the island, grateful for the exertions which the republicans and the *Amis ds Noirs* had made on their behalf, attached themselves to the side of the commissioners, and the republic which they represented. It may naturally be supposed that the blacks would attach themselves to the same party – to the party of those whose watchwords were liberty and equality, and, consequently, were the sworn enemies of slavery; but such was not the case. Considerable numbers of the negroes, it is true, were gained over to the cause of the French republic by the manifesto the commissioners had published abolishing slavery; but the bulk of them kept aloof, and constituted a separate negro army. Strangely enough, this army declared itself anti-republican. Before the death of Louis XVI, the blacks had come to entertain a strong sympathy with the king, and a violent dislike to the republicans. This may have been owing either to the policy of their leaders, François and Biassou, or to the simple fact that the blacks had suffered much at the hands of republican whites. At all events the negro armies called themselves the armies of the king while he was alive; and after he was dead they refused to consider themselves subjects of the republic. In these circumstances, one would be apt to fancy they would side with the British when they landed on the island. But it must be remembered that, along with the blind and unintelligent royalism of the negroes, they were animated by a far stronger and far more real feeling, namely, the desire of freedom and the horror of again being subjected to slavery; and this would very effectually prevent their assisting the British. If they did so, they would be only changing their masters; St Domingo would become a British colony, and they, like the negroes of Jamaica, would become slaves of British planters. No; it was liberty they wanted, and the British would not give them that. They hung aloof, therefore, not acting consistently with the French, much less with the British, but watching the course of events, and ready, at any given moment, to precipitate themselves into the contest and strike a blow for negro independence.

The negroes, however, in the meantime had the fancy to call themselves royalists, François having assumed the title of grand admiral of France and Biassou that of generalissimo of the conquered districts. Toussaint held a military command under them, and acted also as army physician. Every day his influence over the negroes was extending; and as jealousy is a negro vice as well as a European, François became so envious of Toussaint's growing reputation as to cast him into prison, apparently with the further purpose of destroying him. Toussaint, however, was released by Biassou, who, although described as a monster of cruelty, appears to have had some sparks of generous feeling. Shortly after this, Biassou's drunken ferocity rendered it necessary to deprive him of all command, and François and Toussaint became joint-leaders, Toussaint acting in the capacity of lieutenant-general, and François in that of general-in-chief, The negro army at the time judged it expedient to enter the service of Spain, acting in co-operation with the governor of the Spanish colony in the other end of the island, who had been directed by his government at home to carry on war against the French commissioners. The commissioners, it appears, following up the proclamation of liberty to the blacks, which they had published with the hope of increasing their forces sufficiently to resist the British invasion, made an attempt to gain over François and Toussaint. Toussaint, who though himself bound to assign his reasons for refusing to join them, sent an answer which has been preserved. 'We cannot,' he says, 'conform to the will of the nation, because, since the world began, we have never yielded to the will of any but a king. We have lost our French one; so we adopt the king of Spain, who is exceedingly kind to us; and therefore, gentlemen commissioners, we can have nothing to say to you till you put a king on the throne.' This royalist enthusiasm was evidently a mere fancy, which had been put into the heads of the negroes by those who supplied them with words, and which Toussaint allowed himself to be carried away with; and the probability is, that the letter we have quoted was the composition of a Spanish priest. At all events, Toussaint was for some time an officer in the Spanish service, acting under the directions of Joachim Garcia, the president of the Spanish colonial council. In this capacity he distinguished himself greatly. With 600 men, he beat a body of 1500 French out of a strong post which they had occupied near the Spanish town of St Raphael; and afterwards he took in succession the villages of Marmelade, Henneri, Plaisance, and Gonaives. To assist him in these military operations, we are told in some curious notes written by his son, 'that, imitating the example of the captains of antiquity, Lucullus, Pompey, Caesar, and others, he constructed a topographical chart of that part of the island, marking accurately the positions of the hills, the course of the streams,' &c. So much did he harass the commissioners, that one of them, Polverel, in speaking of him after the capture of Marmelade, used the expression: *'Cet homme fait ouverture par tout'* (That man makes an opening everywhere). This expression getting abroad was the cause of Toussaint being afterwards called by the name of *Toussaint l'Ouverture*; which may be translated, Toussaint the Opener; and Toussaint himself knew the value of a good name too well to disclaim the flattering addition. Besides this testimony from an enemy, the negro chief received many marks of favour from the Spanish general, the Marquis d'Hermona. He was appointed lieutenant-general of the army and presented at the same time with a sword and a badge of honour in the name of his Catholic majesty. But the Marquis d'Hermona having been succeeded in the command by another, Toussaint began to find his services less appreciated. His old rival, François, did his best to undermine his influence among the Spaniards; nay, it is said, laid a plot for his assassination, which Toussaint narrowly escaped. He had to complain also of the bad treatment which certain French officers, who had surrendered to him, and whom he had persuaded to accept a command under him, had received at the hands of the Spaniards. All these circumstances operated on the mind of Toussaint, and shook the principles on which he had hitherto acted. While hesitating with respect to his next movements, intelligence of the decree of the French Convention of the 4th February 1794, by which the abolition of negro slavery was confirmed, reached St Domingo; and this immediately decided the step he should take. Quitting the Spanish service, he joined the French general, Laveaux, who – the commissioners Santhonax and Polverel having been recalled – was now invested with the sole governorship of the colony; took the oath of fidelity to the French republic; and being elevated to the rank of brigadier-general, assisted Laveaux in his efforts to drive the English troops out of the island.

In his new capacity, Toussaint was no less successful than he had been while fighting under the Spanish colours. In many engagements, both with the British and the Spaniards, he rendered signal services to the cause of the French. At first, however the French commander, Laveaux, shewed little disposition to place confidence in him; and we can easily conceive that it must have been by slow degrees that a man in the position of Laveaux came to appreciate the character of this negro officer. Laveaux had a task to fulfil; nothing less, in fact, than the task of being the first European to do justice in practice to the negro character, and to treat a negro chief exactly as he would treat a European gentleman. Philosophers, such as the Abbé Gregoire and the Abbé Raynal, had indeed written books to prove that ability and worth were to be found among the negroes, and had laid it down as a maxim that a negro was to be treated like any other man whose circumstances were the same; but probably Laveaux was the first European who felt himself called upon to put the maxim in practice, at least in affairs of any importance. It is highly creditable, therefore, to this French officer, that when he came to have more experience of Toussaint l'Ouverture, he discerned his extraordinary abilities, and esteemed him as much as if he had been a French gentleman educated in the school of Paris. The immediate occasion of the change of the sentiments of Laveaux towards Toussaint was as follows: In the month of March 1795, an insurrection of mulattoes occurred at the town of the Cape, and Laveaux was seized and placed in confinement. On hearing this, Toussaint marched at the head of 10,000 blacks to the town, obliged the inhabitants to open the gates by the threat of a seige, entered in triumph, released the french commander, and reinstated him in his office. In gratitude for this act of loyalty, Laveaux appointed Toussaint lieutenant-governor of the colony, declaring his resolution at the same time to act by his advice in all matters, whether military or civil – a resolution the wisdom of which will appear when we reflect that Toussaint was the only man in the island who could govern the blacks. A saying of Laveaux is also recorded, which shews what a decided opinion he had formed of Toussaint's abilities: 'It is this black,' said he, 'this Spartacus predicted by Raynal, who is destined to avenge the wrongs done to his race.'

A wonderful improvement soon followed the appointment of l'Ouverture as lieutenant-governor of the colony. The blacks, obedient to their champion, were reduced under strict military discipline, and submitted to all the regulations of orderly, civil government. 'It must be allowed,' says General de Lacroix, in his memoirs of the revolution in St Domingo, an account by no means favourable to the blacks – 'it must be allowed that if St Domingo still carried the colours of France, it was solely owing to an old negro, who seemed to bear a commission from Heaven to unite its dilacerated members.' It tended also to promote the cause of good order in the island, that about this time a treaty was concluded between the French Convention and the Spanish government, in consequence of which the war between the French colonists in one end of the island and the Spanish colonists in the other, was at an end, and the only enemy with whom the French commander had still to contend was the British, posted here and there along the coast. On the conclusion of this treaty, Jean François, the former rival of Toussaint, left the island, and Toussaint was therefore without a rival to dispute his authority among the blacks. He employed himself now in attacking the English positions on the west coast, and with such vigour and success, that in a short time he forced them to evacuate all the country on both sides of the river Artibonite, although they still lingered in other parts of the island, from which they could not be dislodged.

Since the departure of the commissioners, Santhonax and Polverel, the whole authority of the colony, both civil and military, had been in the hands of Laveaux; but in the end of the year 1795, a new commission arrived from the mother-country. At the head of this commission was Santhonax, and his colleagues were Giraud, Raymond and Leblanc. The new commissioners, according to their instructions, overwhelmed Toussaint with thanks and compliments; told him he had made the French republic his everlasting debtor, and encouraged him to persevere in his efforts to rid the island of the British. Shortly afterwards, Laveaux, being nominated a member of the legislature, was obliged to return to France; and in the month of April 1796, Toussaint l'Ouverture was appointed his successor, as commander-in-chief of the French forces in St Domingo. Thus, by a remarkable succession of circumstances, was this negro, at the age of fifty-three years, fifty of which had been passed in a state of slavery, placed in the most important position in the island.

Toussaint now began to see his way more clearly, and to become conscious of the duty which Providence had assigned him. Taking all things into consideration, he resolved on being no longer a tool of foreign governments, but to strike a grand blow for the permanent independence of his race. To accomplish this object, he felt that it was necessary to assume and retain, at least for a time, the supreme civil as well as military command. Immediately, therefore, on becoming commander-in-chief in St Domingo, he adopted measures for removing all obstructions to the exercise of his own authority. General Rochambeau had been sent from France with a military command similar to that which Laveaux had held; but finding himself a mere cipher, he became unruly, and Toussaint instantly sent him home. Santhonax the commissioner, too, was an obstacle in the way; and Toussaint, after taking the precaution of ascertaining that he would be able to enforce obedience, got rid of him by the delicate pretext of making him the bearer of dispatches to the Directory. Along with Santhonax, several other officious personages were sent to France; the only person of any official consequence who was retained being the commissioner Raymond, who was a mulatto, and might be useful. As these measures, however, might draw down the vengeance of the

Directory, if not accompanied by some proofs of good-will to France, Toussaint sent two of his sons to Paris to be educated, assuring the Directory at the same time that, in removing Santhonax and his coadjutors, he had been acting for the best interests of the colony. 'I guarantee,' he wrote to the Directory, 'on my own personal responsibility, the orderly behaviour and the good-will to France of my brethren the blacks. You may depend, citizen directors, on happy results; and you shall soon see whether I engage in vain my credit and your hopes.'

The people of Paris received with a generous astonishment the intelligence of the doings of the negro prodigy, and the interest they took in the novelty of the case prevented them from being angry. The Directory, however, judged it prudent to send out General Hedouville, an able and moderate man, to superintend Toussaint's proceedings, and restrain his boldness. When Hedouville arrived at St Domingo, Toussaint went on board the ship to bid him welcome. Conversing with him in the presence of the ship's officers, Toussaint said something about the fatigues of government, upon which the captain of the vessel, meaning to pay him a compliment, said that he wished no greater honour than that of carrying him to France. 'Your ship,' replied Toussaint, too hastily to consider whether what he said was in the best taste – 'your ship is not large enough.' He improved the saying, however, when one of Hedouville's staff made an observation some time afterwards to the same effect, hinting that he should now give up the cares of government and retire to France, to spend his declining years in peace. 'That is what I intend,' said he; 'but I am waiting till this shrub (pointing to a little plant in the ground) grows big enough to make a ship.' Hedouville found himself a mere shadow. Toussaint, though strictly polite to him, paid no attention to his wishes or representations, except when they agreed with his own intentions.

In the meantime, Toussaint was fulfilling his pledge to the Directory, by managing the affairs of the colony with the utmost skill and prudence. One thing, however, still remained to be done, and that was to clear the island of the British troops. Toussaint's exertions had for some time been directed to this end, and with such success, that Saint Mark, Port-au-Prince, Jeremie, and Molé were the only places of which the British still retained possession. He was preparing to attack them in these their last holds, when General Maitland, seeing the hopelessness of continuing an enterprise which had already cost so many British lives, opened a negotiation with him, which ended in a treaty for the evacuation of the island. While General Maitland was making his preparations for quitting the island, Toussaint and he were mutual in their expressions of regard. Toussaint visited the English general, was received with all the pomp of military ceremonial, and, after a splendid entertainment, was presented, in the name of the king of Great Britain, with a costly service of plate and two brass cannons. General Maitland, previous to the embarkation of his troops, visited Toussaint's camp in return, travelling with only three attendants through a tract of country filled with armed blacks. While on his way, he was informed that Roume, the French commissioner, had written to Toussaint, advising him to give a proof of his zeal in the French cause by seizing General Maitland, and detaining him as a prisoner; but confiding in the negro's honour, he did not hesitate to proceed. Arrived at Toussaint's quarters, he had to wait some time before seeing him. At length Toussaint made his appearance, holding in his hands two letters. 'Here general,' he said on entering, 'before we say a word about anything else, read these; the one is a letter I have received from the French commissary, the other is the answer I am just going to despatch.' It is said by French historians that about this time offers were made to Toussaint, on the part of Great Britain, to recognise him as king of Hayti, on condition of his signing a treaty of exclusive commerce with British subjects. It is certain, at least, that if this offer was made, the negro chief did not accept it.

The evacuation of St Domingo by the English in 1798 did not remove all Toussaint's difficulties. The mulattoes, influenced partly by a rumour that the French Directory meditated the re-establishment of the exploded distinction of colour, partly by a jealous dislike to the ascendancy which a pure negro had gained in the colony rose in insurrection under the leadership of Rigaud and Petion, two able and educated mulattoes. The insurrection was formidable; but, by a judicious mingling of severity with caution, Toussaint quelled it, reducing Rigaud and Petion to extremities; and the arrival of a deputation from France in the year 1799, bringing a confirmation of his authority as commander-in-chief in St Domingo by the man who, under the title of First Consul, had superseded the Directory, and now swayed the destinies of France, rendered his triumph complete. Petion and Rigaud, deserted by their adherents, and despairing of any further attempt to shake Toussaint's power, embarked for France.

Confirmed by Bonaparte in the powers which he had for some time been wielding in the colony with such good effect, Toussaint now paid exclusive attention to the internal affairs of the island. In the words of a French biographer, 'he laid the foundation of a new state with the foresight of a mind that could discern what would decay and what would endure. St Domingo rose from its ashes; the reign of law and justice was established; those who had been slaves were now citizens. Religion again reared her altars; and on the sites of ruins were built new edifices.' Certain interesting particulars are also recorded, which give us a better idea of his habits and the nature of his government than these general descriptions. To establish discipline among his black troops, he gave all his superior officers the power of life and death over the subalterns: every superior officer 'commanded with a pistol in his hand.' In all cases where the original possessors of estates which had fallen vacant in the course of the troubles of the past nine years could be traced, they were invited to return and resume their property. Toussaint's great aim was to accustom the negroes to industrious habits. It was only by diligent agriculture, he said, that the blacks could ever raise themselves. Accordingly, while every trace of personal slavery was abolished, he took means to compel the negroes to work as diligently as ever they had done under the whip of their overseers. All those plantations the proprietors of which did not reappear were lotted out among the negroes, who, as a remuneration for their labour, received one-third of the produce, the rest going to the public revenue. There were as yet no civil or police courts which could punish idleness or vagrancy, but the same purpose was served by courts-martial. The ports of the island were opened to foreign vessels, and every encouragement held out to traffic. In consequence of these arrangements, a most surprising change took place: the plantations were again covered with crops; the sugar-houses and distilleries were rebuilt; the export trade began to revive; and the population, orderly and well behaved, began to increase. In addition to these external evidences of good government, the island exhibited those finer evidences which consist in mental culture and civilisation of manners. Schools were established, and books became common articles in the cottages of the negro labourers. Music and the theatre were encouraged; and public worship was conducted with all the usual pomp of the Romish church. The whites, the mulattoes, and the blacks mingled in the same society, and exchanged with each other all the courtesies of civilised intercourse. The commander-in-chief himself set the example by holding public levees, at which, surrounded by his officers, he received the visits of the principal colonists; and his private parties, it is said, 'might have vied with the best regulated societies of Paris.' Himself frugal and abstemious in his habits, he studied magnificence in all matters of court arrangement, the dress of his officers, his furniture, his entertainments, &c. His attention to decorum might be thought excessive, unless we knew the state of manners which had prevailed in St Domingo while it was a French colony. He would never allow the white ladies to appear at his court with their necks uncovered: women, he said, should always look as if they were going to church. Like every man in high office, Toussaint was frequently annoyed by ambitious persons applying to him for situations for which they had no capacity. He had the art, it is said, of sending such persons away without offending them. A negro, for instance, who thought he had some claim to his acquaintanceship, would come and ask to be appointed a judge or a magistrate.

'Oh yes,' Toussaint would reply, as if complying with the request; and then he would add: 'Of course you understand Latin?'

'Latin!' the suitor would say; 'no general, I never learnt it.'

'What!' Toussaint would exclaim, 'not know Latin, and yet want to be a magistrate!' And then he would pour out a quantity of gibberish, intermingled with as many Latin sounding words as he could remember; and the candidate, astonished at such a display of learning, would go away disappointed, of course, at not getting the office, but laying all the blame upon his ignorance of Latin.

§

Successful in all his schemes of improvement, Toussaint had only one serious cause for dread. While he admired, and, it may be, imitated Napoleon Bonaparte, he entertained a secret fear of the projects of that great general. Although Bonaparte, as first consul, had confirmed him in his command, several circumstances had occurred to excite alarm. He had sent two letters to Bonaparte, both headed: 'The First of the Blacks to the First of the Whites,' one of which announced the complete pacification of the island, and requested the ratification of certain appointments which he had made, and the other explained his reasons for cashiering a French official; but to these letters Bonaparte had not deigned to return an answer. Moreover, the representatives from St Domingo had been excluded from the French senate; and rumours had reached the island that the first consul meditated the re-establishment of slavery. Toussaint thought it advisable, in this state of matters, to be before-hand with the French consul in forming a constitution for the island, to supersede the military government with which it had hitherto been content. A draft of a constitution was accordingly drawn up by his directions, and with the assistance of the ablest Frenchmen in the island; and after being submitted to an assembly of representatives from all parts of St Domingo, it was formally published on the 1st of July 1801. By this constitution the whole executive of the island, with the command

174

of the forces, was to be intrusted to a governor-general. Toussaint was appointed governor-general for life; his successors were to hold office for five years each; and he was to have the power of nominating the first of them. Various other provisions were contained in the constitution, and its general effect was to give St Domingo a virtual independence, under the guardianship of France.

Not disheartened by the taciturnity of Bonaparte, Toussaint again addressed him in respectful terms, and entreated his ratification of the new constitution. The first consul, however, had already formed the resolution of extinguishing Toussaint and taking possession of St Domingo; and the conclusion of a treaty of peace with England (1st October 1801) increased his haste to effect the execution of his deceitful purpose. In vain did persons acquainted with the state of the island endeavour to dissuade him from this movement, by representing the evils which would arise. 'I want,' he said to the minister Forfeit, who was one of those who reasoned with him on the subject – 'I want, I tell you, to get rid of 60,000 men.' This was probably the secret of his determination to invade St Domingo. Now that the treaty with England was concluded, he felt the presence of so many of his old companions in arms to be an encumbrance. There were men among them very likely to criticise his government and thwart his designs, and these it would be very convenient to send on a distant expedition. Nay more, it would not be misrepresenting Napoleon's character, if we were to suppose that some jealousy of his negro admirer mingled with his other views. Be this as it may, the expedition was equipped. It consisted of twenty-six ships-of-war and a number of transports, carrying an army of 25,000 men, the flower of the French troops, who embarked reluctantly. The command of the army was given to General Leclerc, the husband of Pauline Bonaparte, the consul's sister. Bonaparte had never forgiven his sister this marriage with a man of low birth; and it is said that a frequent cause of annoyance to him, in the first years of his consulship, was the arrival in Paris of all sorts of odd people from the country, who, being relations of Leclerc, claimed to be the kinsmen of the first consul. Bonaparte accordingly took this opportunity of sending his brother-in-law abroad. Leclerc was accompanied by his wife Pauline, a woman who, to a strength of mind worthy of Napoleon's sister, added a large share of personal beauty. Many of Toussaint's enemies accompanied Leclerc in this expedition, among whom we may mention Rochambeau, who was second in command, and the mulattoes Rigaud and Petion.

The French squadron reached St Domingo on the 29th of January 1802. 'We are lost,' said Toussaint, when he saw the ships approach;

'all France is coming to St Domingo.' The invading army was divided into four bodies. General Kervesau with one, was to take possession of the Spanish town of St Domingo; General Rochambeau, with another, was to march on Fort Dauphin; General Boudet, with a third, on Port-au-Prince; and Leclerc himself, with the remainder, on Cape François. In all quarters the French were successful in effecting a landing. Rochambeau, in landing with his division, came to an engagement with the blacks who had gathered on the beach, and slaughtered a great number of them. At Cape François, Leclerc sent an intimidating message to Christophe, the negro whom Toussaint had stationed there as commander; but the negro replied that he was responsible only to Toussaint, his commander-in-chief. Perceiving, however, that his post was untenable, owing to the inclination of white inhabitants of the town to admit Leclerc, Christophe set fire to the houses at night, and retreated to the hills by the light of the conflagration, carrying 2000 whites with him as hostages.

Although the French had effected a landing, the object of the invasion was yet far from being attained. Toussaint and the blacks had retired to the interior, and, in fastness where no military force could reach them, they were preparing for future attacks. Sensing that the force of language might not be wanting to co-operate with the force of arms, the first consul had sent out a proclamation to be distributed among the inhabitants of St Domingo, assuring them that, 'whatever was their origin or their colour, they were all equal, all free, all French in the eyes of God and the republic; that France herself, long desolated by civil wars, but now at peace with the universe, had sent her ships to guarantee civil liberty in St Domingo: but that if anger of the republic were provoked, it would devour her enemies as the fire devours the dried sugar-canes.' The proclamation did not produce the intended effect; the blacks still refused to submit. Another stroke of policy was in reserve, the intention of which was to incline Toussaint himself to forbear his opposition to the occupation of the island by the French. Our readers already know that two of Toussaint's sons, whose names were Issac and Placide, had been sent to Paris to be educated. At Paris, they were placed under the tuition of one M. Coasnon. The first consul resolved that Toussaint's two sons, along with their preceptor, should accompany the expedition under Leclerc to St Domingo, to try the effect which the sight of them might have on the mind of the negro chief. He had sent for them at the Tuileries, and received them very graciously, inquiring of M. Coasnon which was Issac and which Placide. 'Your father,' he said to them, 'is a great man, and has rendered many services to France. Tell

Toussaint l'ouverture
1743 – 1803

Henri Christophe
1767 – 1820

him I said so; and tell him not to believe that I have any hostile intentions against St Domingo. The troops I send are not destined to fight against the native troops but to increase their strength. The man I have appointed commander is my own brother-in-law.' He then asked them some questions in mathematics; and the young men withdrew, delighted with the first consul's kindness. After landing at Cape François, Leclerc despatched Coasnon with Toussaint's two sons to the village of Henneri, where he heard that Toussaint then was. One of the sons, Issac, has written an account of this interview with his father, and of the transactions which followed it. Travelling to Henneri, he tells us, with M. Coasnon, the negroes everywhere on the road received them with raptures. When they reached Henneri, Toussaint was absent and they spent the first evening with their mother and the rest of the family. Next day Toussaint joined them, and meeting him at the door, they threw themselves into his arms. M. Coasnon then presented him with a letter from the first consul, which he read on the spot. The letter was a skilful mixture of flattery and menace:

'If the French flag floats over St Domingo, it is owing to you and your brave blacks. Called by your abilities and the force of circumstances to the first command in the island, you have put an end to civil war, and brought back into repute religion and the worship of God, from whom everything proceeds. The constitution which you have made contains a number of excellent things; but....'

There then followed a few threatening passages. After reading the letter, Toussaint turned to Coasnon and said: 'Which am I to believe? – the first consul's words, or General Leclerc's actions? The first consul offers me peace; and yet General Leclerc no sooner arrives than he rushes into a war with us. However, I shall write to General Leclerc. An attempt was then made to influence him through his paternal feelings; but at length Toussaint put an end to the interview by saying: 'Take back my sons,' and immediately rode off.

The correspondence which Toussaint entered into with Leclerc produced no good result, and the war began in earnest. Toussaint and Christophe were declared outlaws, and battle after battle was fought with varying success. The mountainous nature of the interior greatly impeded the progress of the French. The Alps themselves, Leclerc said, were not nearly so troublesome to a military man as the hills of St Domingo. On the whole, however, the advantage was decidedly on the side of the French; and the blacks were driven by degrees out of all their principal positions. The success of the French was not entirely the consequence of their military skill and valour; it was partly owing also to the effect which the proclamations of Leclerc had on the minds of the negroes and their commanders. If they were to enjoy the perfect liberty which these proclamations promised them, if they were to continue free men as they were now, what mattered it whether the French were in possession of the island or not? Such was the general feeling; and accordingly many of Toussaint's most eminent officers, among whom were Laplume and Maurepas, went over to the French. Deserted thus by many of his officers and by the great mass of the negro population, Toussaint, supported by his two bravest and ablest generals, Dessalines and Christophe, still held out, and protracted the war. Dessalines, besieged in the fort of Crete à Pierrot by Leclerc and nearly the whole of the french army, did not give up the defence until he had caused the loss of his besiegers of about 3000 men, including several distinguished officers; and even then, rushing out, he fought his way through the enemy, and made good his retreat.

The reduction of the fortress of Crete à Pierrot was considered decisive of the fate of the war; and Leclerc, deeming dissimulation no longer necessary, permitted many negroes to be massacred, and issued an order virtually re-establishing the power of the old French colonists over their slaves. This rash step opened the eyes of the negroes who had joined the French: they deserted in masses; Toussaint was again at the head of an army; and Leclerc was in danger of losing all the fruits of his past labours, and being obliged to begin his enterprise over again. This was a very disagreeable prospect; for although strong reinforcements were arriving from France, the disorders incident to military life in a new climate were making large incisions into his army. He resolved, therefore, to fall back on his former policy; and on the 25th of April 1802, he issued a proclamation directly opposite in this spirit to his former order, asserting the equality of the various races, and holding out the prospect of full citizenship to the blacks. The negroes were again deceived, and again deserted Toussaint. Christophe, too, despairing of any farther success against the French, entered into negotiation with Leclerc, securing as honourable terms, as could be desired. The example of Christophe was imitated by Dessalines, and by Paul l'Ouverture, Toussaint's brother. Toussaint, thus left alone was obliged to submit; and Christophe, in securing good terms for himself, had not neglected the opportunity of obtaining similar advantages for his commander-in-chief. On the 1st of May 1802, a treaty was concluded between Leclerc and Toussaint l'Ouverture, the conditions of which were, that Toussaint should continue to govern St Domingo as hitherto, Leclerc acting only in the capacity of French deputy, and that all the officers in Toussaint's army should be allowed to retain their respective ranks. 'I swear,' added Leclerc, 'before the Supreme Being, to respect the liberty of the people of St Domingo.' Thus the war appeared to have reached a happy close; the whites and blacks mingled with each other once more as friends; and Toussaint retired to one of his estates near Gonaives, to lead a life of quiet domestic enjoyment.

The instructions of the first consul, however, had been precise, that the negro chief should be sent as a prisoner to France. Many reasons recommended such a step as more likely than any other to break the spirit of independence among the blacks, and rivet the French power in the island. The expedition had been one of the most disastrous that France had ever undertaken. A pestilence resembling the yellow fever, but more fatal and terrible than even that dreadful distemper, had swept many thousands of the French to their graves. What with the ravages of the plague, and the losses in war, it was calculated that 30,000 men, 1500 officers of various ranks – among whom were fourteen generals – and 700 physicians and surgeons, perished in the expedition.

It is our melancholy duty now to record one of the blackest acts committed by Napoleon. Agreeably to his orders, the person of Toussaint was treacherously arrested, while residing peacefully in his house near Gonaives. Two negro chiefs who endeavoured to rescue him were killed on the spot, and a large number f his friends were at the same time made prisoners. The fate of many of these was never known; but Toussaint himself, his wife, and all his family, were carried at midnight on board the *Hero* man-of-war, then in the harbour, which immediately set sail for France. After a short passage of twenty-five days, the vessel arrived at Brest (June 1802); and here Toussaint took his last leave of his wife and family. They were sent to Bayonne; but by the orders of the first consul, he was carried to the château of Joux, in the east of France, among the Jura mountains. Placed in this bleak and dismal region, so different from the tropical climate to which he had been accustomed, his sufferings may easily imagined. Not satisfied, however, with confining his unhappy prisoner to the fortress generally, Bonaparte enjoined that he should be secluded in a dungeon, and denied anything beyond the plainest necessaries of existence. For the first few months of his captivity, Toussaint was allowed to be attended by a faithful negro servant; but at length this single attendant was removed, and he was left alone in his misery and despair. It appears a rumour had gone abroad that Toussaint, during the war in St Domingo, had buried a large amount of treasure in the earth; and during his captivity at joux, an officer was sent by the first consul to interrogate him respecting the place where he had concealed it. 'The treasures I have lost,' said Toussaint, 'are not those which you seek.' After an imprisonment of ten months, the negro was found dead in his dungeon on the 27th of April 1803. He was sitting at the side of the fireplace, with his hands resting on his legs, and his head drooping. The account given at the time was, that he had died of apoplexy; but some authors have not hesitated to ascribe it to less natural circumstances. 'The governor of the fort,' observes one French writer, 'made two excursions to Neufchâtel, in Switzerland. The first time, he left the keys of the dungeons with a captain whom he chose to act for him during his absence. The captain accordingly had occasion to visit Toussaint, who conversed with him about his past life, and expressed his indignation at the design imputed to him by the first consul, of having wished to betray St Domingo to the English. As Toussaint, reduced to a scanty farinaceous diet, suffered greatly from the want of coffee, to which he had been accustomed, the captain generously procured it for him. This first absence of the governor of the fort, however, was only an experiment. It was not long before he left the fort again, and this time he said, with a mysterious, unquiet air, to the captain: 'I leave you in charge of the fort, but I do not give you the keys to the dungeons; the prisoners do not require anything.' Four days after, he returned, and Toussaint was dead – starved.' According to another account, this miserable victim of despotism, and against whom there was no formal or reasonable charge, was poisoned; but this rests on no credible testimony,m and there is reason to believe that Toussaint died a victim only to the severities of confinement in this inhospitable prison. This melancholy termination to his sufferings took place when he was sixty years of age.

Toussaint's family continued to reside in France. They were removed from Bayonne to Agen, and here one of the younger sons of Toussaint died soon after his father. Toussaint's wife died in May 1816, in the arms of her sons Issac and Placide. In 1825, Issac l'Ouverture wrote a brief memoir of his father, to which we acknowledge ourselves to have been indebted.

Current Number	By what Ship, or how taken.	Time when.	Prizes Names.	Whether Man of War, Privateer or Merchant Vessel	Of what Co...
2667			L'veillée	Priv	Hav...
2668			D	D	
2669			Le Calvados	Priv	
2670			D	D	
2671	Unicorn	June 8. 96	La Tribune	Frigate	
2672			L'Agricole	D	
2673			Le Cigne	Cutter	
2674			D	D	West...
2675			Le Calvados	Priv	
2676			Le Cigne	Cutter	
2677			D	D	
2678			Le Terrible	Priv	
2679			Dumourier	Priv	
2680			La Thamis	Frigate	
2681	Granada & St Vincent		London		France
2682					
2683					West Indies
2684					Africa
2685					West Indies
2686					Africa
2687					
2688					
2689					West Indies
2690					France
2691					West Indies

Prisoners Names.	Quality.	Time when received into Custody.	Ex. D. U.D. or Ef.	Time when.	How disposed of, and by what Order.
Fran.ᵒⁱˢ Feron	Prize Mast.ʳ	Nov. 29. 1796	D	Jan.ʸ 19. 1798	Smallbridge Castle
Julien Marchand	Servant		D	Dec.ʳ 31. 1790	Of Provenance
Jean Jos. Sicard	Lieut.ᵗ		D	16 March 1799	Of Oxfford
Ant.ᵒ Raybaud	Surgeon		D	Dec.ʳ 31. 1790	Of Provenance
Fran.ᵒ Fonteneau	Servant		D	Dec 26. 1796	On Parole to the Ship by orders of the Board
Jean Bap.ᵗ Nicolleau	Guard. Marine		Er	July 3. 1797	
Mathurin Galligan	Servant		D	Sept.ʳ 13. 1799	Of Provenance
Fran.ᵒ Richecœur	Mousse		D	Jan.ʸ 17. 1800	Of France
Jean Vallery Becquet	Lieut.ᵗ		D	16 March 1799	Of Oxfford
Fran.ᵒ Cottonce	Mousse				
Raoul Dagaud	Seaman		See Vol 2.ⁿᵈ		
Louis Le Grand	Mousse				
Jean Courval	Servant		D	Mar.ʳ 28. 1799	Of Provenance
Jean Gorse	Sailmaker		D	Dec.ʳ 8.ᵗʰ 1796	On parole to the Chippenham
Dumat	Soldier	Dec.ʳ 2.ᵈ 1796	UD	April 3. 1797	Hospital
Lara	D.ᵒ		D	Jan.ʸ 19. 98	Smallbridge Castle
De Grave	Mulatto Slave		D.ᵒ	d.ᵒ	d.ᵒ
Sauchagrave	D.ᵒ		D.ᵒ	d.ᵒ	d.ᵒ
La Combe	Mulatto Slave		D.ᵒ	d.ᵒ	d.ᵒ
La Vesture	Negro Slave		d.ᵒ	d.ᵒ	d.ᵒ
Hela	D.ᵒ		D.ᵒ	d.ᵒ	d.ᵒ
Felis	D.ᵒ		D.ᵒ	d.ᵒ	d.ᵒ
Ojeux	Mulatto Slave		d.ᵒ	d.ᵒ	d.ᵒ
Charles	Soldier		d.ᵒ	d.ᵒ	d.ᵒ
Bulau	Mulatto Slave		d.ᵒ	d.ᵒ	d.ᵒ

Current Number	By what Ship, or how taken.	Time when.	Prizes Names.	Whether Man of War, Privateer, or Merchant Vessel	Of what Country
2692	Granada & St. Vincent				West Indies
2693					Africa
2694					West Indies
2695					Africa
2696					
2697					
2698					
2699					
2700					
2701					West Indies
2702					Africa
2703					West Indies
2704					Do.
2705					Africa
2706					France
2707					West Indies
2708					Do.
2709					Africa
2710					France
2711					
2712			Labricur		
2713					
2714					
2715			Bucaonfaite		

Prisoners Names.	Quality.	Time when received into Custody.	Ex. D. D.D. or Ef.	Time when.	How disposed of, and by what Order.
Joseph	Mulatto Slave	Dec. 4. 1796	D	Jan 19th 1798	f. Smallbridge Cartel
Dominique	Negro Slave		D	do	do
Victor	Mulatto Slave		DD	22 Dec 1796	in the Hospital
Paschal	Negro Slave		D	Jan 19 1798	f. Smallbridge Cartel
Lesperance	Do		D	do	do
Andee	Do		DD	Oct 12. 1797	f Nancy Cartel
Jaques	Do		D	Jan 19 1798	f. Smallbridge Cartel
Lindau	Do		D	do	do
Timothee	Do		DD	Oct 12. 1797	f Nancy Cartel
Pierre	Mulatto Slave		DD	Jany 15 1790	Hospital
Michael	Negro Slave		D	Jan 19 1798	f. Smallbridge Cartel
La Tainte	Mulatto Slave		D	do	do
Baboud	Do		D	do	do
Pierre	Negro Slave		D	do	do
Biardelle	Soldier		DD	18 Feby 1797	in the Hospital
Pepierre	Mulatto Slave		D	Jan 19th 1798	f. Smallbridge Cartel
Boureau	Do		D	do	do
Cadeaux	Negro Slave		D	do	do
Heautaux	Col. Commandant of Fort Charlotte		D	Dec 8th 1796	On Parole to Cap Francois
Madame Heautaux	his Wife		D	do	do
Anthoine de Terré	Seaman	Mar 11 1797	D	Jan 19 1798	f. Smallbridge Cartel
Claud Louville	Lieut	"	DD	April 4. 1799	f Nancy
Claud Lavergne	Lieut	Mar 11. 97	D	May 1797	Pirate to Chipoter...on
Claud R. Grimvell		June 1797	See	Vol 2nd	

Bibliography

Primary Sources

Public Records Office
    Admiralty
    ADM/MT/416 Transport Board.
    ADM 1/ 2894.
    A.D.M 97/98-131.
    A.D.M 98.
    A.D.M99/92-263.
    A.D.M 100/4 and 5
    A.D.M10/14.
    HMS Ganges Log. ADM 1/2131 & ADM 1/2133.

North Devon Athenaeum:
    Sherborne Mercury,1796.
    Exeter Flying Post, 1796.
    Annual register,1796.
    London Gazette 1796.
    London Journal,1796.
    Illustrated London News, 1856.
    North Devon Journal, 1856.
    The Dictionary of National Biography.

Lloyd's list, 1796.

Customs Records, 1796.

National Maritime Museum.

Secondary Sources

Gosse, P.H., *A Naturalist's rambles on the Devonshire Coast.* (1853)

Slade-King, Mrs., *Notes on the Olden Times of Ilfracombe*, Transactions of the Devonshire association, Vol.XI. (1879)

Page, J.L.W., *The Coasts of Devon and Lundy Island.* (1895).

Larn, R., *Devon Shipwrecks* (London, 1974).

Page, R., *Coast of Devon and Lundy*

Marshal, C., *Coin Weights for Gold Coins, Coin Weights for English Coins* (1987). Parts 2-3, T.H.M.May & June .

Sheppard, T. And Musham, J.F., *Money Scales and Weights* (1973)

Steinberg, S.H. *Steinbergs Dictionary of British History.* London.1974

Lamplugh, L. *A History of Ilfracombe.* Chichester (1984)

Chanter, The Reverend John Mill, *Wanderings in North Devon* (1887)

Chambers's Miscellany of Instructive and Entertaining Tracts. Vol. X. c1870.

Ilfracombe Museum:
Old Times in the West Country; Stories Legends, and Highwaymen; Traditions, and Rhymes of Old North Devon. c1873. (The Green Book)

Slade-King, Mrs., *Transactions of the Devonshire Association* Vol.XI. (1879)

Ilfracombe Parish magazine (1904).

Cross, Dr. J.F., *The human skeletal remains from Rapparee Cove* (1997)

Palmer, M.G, *Black note book*

Gosse, P.H.1853. *A Naturalists rambles on the Devonshire Coast*

A large collection of records regarding the wreck of *The London* can be viewed at the Ilfracombe Museum.
OPEN:
April-October
Every DAY 10 AM. to 5.30 PM.

November-March
Monday to Friday
10 AM. to 12.30 PM.
Telephone (01271) 863541.

INDEX